SONS TO SAMUEL

OTHER BOOKS BY THE SAME AUTHOR:

IN METHODIST HISTORY

Family Circle (A Study of the Epworth Household)
John Wesley and the Eighteenth Century
After Wesley
Methodism and England
This Methodism
Adam Clarke
S. E. Keeble: Pioneer and Prophet
The Astonishing Youth (A Portrait of John Wesley)

IN DEVOTIONAL STUDIES

The Coming of the Kingdom
Seeing the Invisible
God and the Sparrow
So Rich a Crown
In the Midst of the Throne

IN SOCIAL STUDIES

One Increasing Purpose (Beckly Lecture, 1947)
Church and Society
The Signs of Our Times (Cato Lecture, 1957)
   Etc.

Sons to Samuel

by

MALDWYN EDWARDS

WIPF & STOCK · Eugene, Oregon

Wipf and Stock Publishers
199 W 8th Ave, Suite 3
Eugene, OR 97401

Sons to Samuel
By Edwards, Maldwyn
Copyright©1961 Methodist Publishing - Epworth Press
ISBN 13: 978-1-4982-0712-6
Publication date 9/18/2014
Previously published by Epworth Press, 1961

Every effort has been made to trace the current copyright owner of this publication but without success. If you have any information or interest in the copyright, please contact the publishers.

FOR

DEAN W. R. CANNON

AND MY FRIENDS AT EMORY

Preface

IN HER BOOK, *Son to Susanna*, Mrs Elsie Harrison was concerned to show the influence over John Wesley of his mother. None would dispute the incalculable influence that she exercised over all her children, and John was ready always to acknowledge the unpayable debt he owed to her. Yet Samuel, the Rector, also played a vital part in shaping the lives of his children, and his influence over his three sons has never been assessed or sufficiently acknowledged.

I have set myself to show the nature and extent of this influence of the father over his three sons, and to demonstrate the special place that the Rector must always have in the beginnings of the Methodist story.

I have shown the relations of the three brothers with each other and, more particularly, the enduring influence that Samuel, junior, exercised over Charles Wesley.

Then I have developed the theme of the dependence of John and Charles upon each other in the progress of the Methodist revival. It has been my aim to bring out the very real and not always acknowledged help that Charles was to brother John, even after he had ceased to be an active itinerant.

I have worked out the partnership of the two

brothers in the unique theological contribution which Methodism has made to the Church universal. They were not only original as thinkers, but, each in his own medium, were able jointly to communicate to the world their new insight into the nature of God's dealings with men.

Finally, I have endeavoured to assess what still remains to justify the continued existence of Methodism as a world Church. I have listed four main features which still characterize Methodism throughout the world and enable it to bring its own distinctive gift into the treasury of the universal Church.

The substance of the book was delivered as the Quillian Lectures in Ministers' Week at Emory University, Georgia, 1959. Three years ago for a short spell I had the privilege of serving on the staff as a Visiting Professor of Church History.

I want to express my indebtedness to the Dean and the members of the Staff of the Theological Faculty in Emory in giving me a fresh chance to visit a place in which I was so happy and received such kindness.

MALDWYN EDWARDS

Contents

	INTRODUCTION	1
1	THE RECTOR OF EPWORTH	5
2	THE THREE BROTHERS	26
3	THE UNALIENABLE FRIENDS	41
4	BROTHERS IN BATTLE	62
5	THE JOINT MANIFESTO	85
6	WHAT REMAINS?	117
	INDEX	133

Acknowledgements

I DESIRE to express my deep sense of appreciation to Mrs Pierce Jones, who has so kindly typed the manuscript, and to Mr Max Ede, who has most painstakingly read through the manuscript and made excellent suggestions.

Now, as ever, I am indebted to my wife for her sustained interest in the writing of the book and in the preparation of the Index.

Note on Books

THE indispensable sources of reference are:
The Journal of John Wesley, 8 Vols. Standard Edition (London, 1909).
The Letters of John Wesley, 8 Vols. Standard Edition (London, 1931).
The Works of John Wesley, 14 Vols. (The 1872 edition is now available, published by Zondervan, *via* Epworth Press.)

For the Rector, one must still return to the—
Life and Times of Samuel Wesley, by Luke Tyerman (London, 1866).
The Wesley Family, by Adam Clarke (London, n.d.) and
Memorials of the Wesley Family, by G. J. Stevenson (London, 1876).

SONS TO SAMUEL

An essential source of information also is—
Original Letters by the Revd. John Wesley and His Friends, edited by Joseph Priestley (1791, London).

The curious will be delighted to read—
Poems on Several Occasions, by Samuel Wesley Junr. (enlarged edition, 1862).

Lives of John Wesley are without number, but the one classic *Life* is that of Robert Southey (London, 1820); and despite its inaccuracies and its hero worship, the *Life and Times of John Wesley* in 3 Vols. by Luke Tyerman (London, 1876, 3rd Edn), is still a useful book of reference. See also *The Life of John Wesley*, by John Telford (London, 1886).

Charles Wesley has never had a worthy biographer, and the *Memoirs* by T. Jackson (London, 1848) must still be used.

The reader must also refer to Charles Wesley's own *Journal* in 2 Vols. (London, n.d.), though it ends, unfortunately, in 1756.

A recent book on John and Charles, *A Tale of Two Brothers*, by Mabel R. Brailsford (London, 1954), may be noticed, but its literary merits are far greater than its religious perception.

PUBLISHER'S NOTE. In the above list of books, Dr Edwards has, with his customary modesty, omitted mention of his *Family Circle* and *The Astonishing Youth*—books which we take the reasonable liberty of commending.

Introduction

IT IS PERHAPS necessary to give a few details about the Epworth household, since this book assumes a certain acquaintance on the part of the reader with the Wesley family.

The Rector and his young wife came to Epworth in 1697 and stayed there until his death in 1735. Even today Epworth is not readily accessible except by road, but in the eighteenth century it was in the midst of the Isle of Axholme. The district was low-lying and surrounded on three sides by the rivers Trent, Don and Idle. Actually, it had been a swamp in the seventeenth century, but some years before the young Rector arrived the land had been drained and gradually it had become rich and fertile. Nevertheless, throughout his whole occupancy of the living he had to contend with floods and with ruined harvests. Even harder for a sensitive spirit to bear was the sullen nature of the people in that remote part of Lincolnshire. For long years they regarded the Rectory family with suspicion and even with active hostility. There are indeed those who contend that the famous rectory fire in 1709 was a malicious act on the part of the townsmen. By sheer patience and industry, however, the Rector gradually won the respect of his parishioners, and when he died the number attending Holy Communion had risen from twenty to over 100. One remarkable fact is that, despite the most discouraging circumstances under which he lived, the Rector was never once known to grumble at his fate or to seem envious of others. His wife said on more than one occasion that with his great gifts he deserved a far greater scope of service, but it never came his way and he never rebelled against his lot. Quite apart from the unending struggle against poverty, life in the rectory was by no means easy. The nineteen children were born in regular succession, though only ten survived infancy, and so much child-bearing coupled with inadequate help in the rectory brought Susanna to a condition of health in which she confessed that she was never free from pain. This must have hung heavily over the Rector's spirit, because, despite superficial criticism of their married life, there is no question that their love for each other was deep and lasting.

There were seven girls, all lovely and talented, and yet, with two exceptions, they all made unhappy marriages. Kezia alone remained unmarried, dying when only thirty-one years of age. Mary, known as Molly, also died young, but she at least had one completely happy year of marriage before she died in childbirth. Apart from Mary, the only daughter who married happily was Nancy, who was wedded to a highly respected land-surveyor. There is one

INTRODUCTION

adequate reason for the wrong choices that the girls made. It was virtually impossible for them in so isolated a Rectory to find suitors who were their equal in birth and breeding, and consequently they had to accept men who were manifestly their inferiors. This was disastrous indeed. The most gifted and perhaps the loveliest of them all was Hetty, and her story has become immortalized in Quiller Couch's novel *Hetty Wesley*. We need in this direful record to remember that Emily and Martha, though both wretched in their married state, were able to free themselves from their husbands, and in both cases to come to London and to assist in the work of the London Methodist Societies. They were both close companions of John; and Emily, for the last thirty years of her life, gave herself completely to the work of Methodism in London. She was the true helpmate that John failed to find in the woman that he married.

When the Rectory is mentioned it is always the incomparable Susanna who springs foremost to the mind. This is understandable, but it produces a wrong perspective. The story of the Rectory can only fully be told when the Rector, equally with his wife, is woven into the drama of the children's lives.

In the following pages the reader will be shown how inestimable was the debt which the sons owed to their father, but it must be confessed that the Rector's pride in the character and accomplishment of his sons caused him to neglect the company of his daughters. A book can properly be written about the Rector and his sons, but no one would write a book with the title 'Daughters to Samuel'. It is doubtful whether he really ever understood them, and certainly in all the correspondence that survives they never speak of him with love but only with respect.

The one outstanding exception to this attitude was Mary, who, because of a fall in childhood, became crippled and was in effect maid-of-all-work at the rectory. With her singular sweetness of disposition she never cavilled against her lot, but made herself indispensable to her father as well as to her mother. For many years she acted as his amanuensis, and her secretarial work must greatly have lightened his labours. There was a deep affection between the Rector and herself, and that throws into relief the lack of a similar spontaneous love on the part of the other girls.

This then is the man whom critics have variously judged, but who, as head of the Epworth household, has made his own imperishable contribution to the Wesley saga.

CHAPTER ONE

The Rector of Epworth

A MAN MIGHT well pray to be delivered from his biographers. In the first period of Methodism, the Rector of Epworth was treated with great respect as the father of John and Charles Wesley. Thus, unhappily, all the blemishes were removed and the figure that emerged was strangely unlike the tempestuous, irascible, and altogether human Samuel who shaped so strongly the fortunes of his family. Today the pendulum has swung to an opposite extreme, and through much staring at the blemishes modern writers have not realized the outstanding qualities of the man.

That he was subject to gusty fits of anger and could be stubborn and self-willed need not be denied. Indeed, it is a matter of great interest that John, whose imperturbability could not even be shaken by a virago of a wife, was so much the son of Susanna the mother, whilst Charles, prone to sudden emotional outbursts, was so much the child of Samuel the father. Yet in neither father nor son was there anything bitter or ungenerous; the squalls were only the surface commotions of deep and affectionate natures. Many attribute the tension in the relationship of Samuel and his wife to the Rector's moods, but in truth the frequent sources of disagreement arose from a compound of difference in temperament, the excessive strain of frequent childbearing, and the Rector's inability to manage his own finances.

This last reason for irritation has been so magnified that a truer perspective is necessary. The emoluments of the living at Epworth were relatively high, and the Rector, like so many country parsons of the eighteenth century, was expected to supplement his income by his farming. But he was a poor farmer, and therefore the income from the benefice and the land together could not match the financial strain of a large and growing family, the charge of repairs, insurance, interest and taxes, and the provision for his children's education. Susanna knew all this and never allowed their many differences of opinion to spoil their married life. When Samuel Annesley, her brother, attacked the Rector's unbusinesslike methods, Susanna defended her husband point by point and declared it 'a thousand pities that a man of his brightness and rare endowments of learning and useful knowledge should be confined to an obscure corner of the country where his talents are buried'. Nor did she leave her brother in any doubt of her fundamental loyalty: 'Where he lives I will live, and where he dies will I die, and there will I be buried. God do so unto me and more also if aught but death part him and me.'

THE RECTOR OF EPWORTH

The Rector's misunderstanding of his daughters is a graver charge which modern biographers level as they contrast the 'cribb'd, cabin'd, and confin'd' life of the girls with the wider opportunities of the boys. But in the eighteenth century it was still a man's world, and Napoleon's *'carrière ouverte aux talents'* certainly never applied to girls. What they could do, the Epworth girls succeeded in doing. No woman could hope for much beyond the work of a governess, teacher, or housekeeper, and these positions the Wesley girls occupied according to their talents and inclinations. Their education, though largely acquired at home, gave them those accomplishments which were so carefully set out in the prospectuses of fashionable boarding-schools. The need was 'to sing and play the harpsichord and guitar': 'to be instructed in reading, the art of good penmanship, the casting of accounts and embroidery'. All the Wesley sisters could read and write well, as their letters show; Hetty indeed knew Latin and some Greek, and could write verses for the *Gentleman's Magazine;* John could say of Emily that she was the best reader of Milton he had ever heard; and Martha was a valued member of Dr Samuel Johnson's literary circle.

The gravamen of criticism lies in the Rector's treatment of Hetty, the cleverest and most unhappy of them all. It is now confirmed that Hetty returned in disillusionment from her clandestine elopement.

She was pregnant, and when this was discovered alarm was added to reproach and Susanna sided with the Rector in deciding that Hetty must marry the first suitor who would offer his hand in marriage. Only Mary and the three brothers survive a twentieth-century criticism of family relationships; the others in varying degrees were children of their century. This is not to discharge the Rector from serious blame, but to say that he was not alone at the Rectory in his attitude. In his case popular prejudice has been strengthened by the fact that the rigid ecclesiastic gained a victory over the father. This is a glaring instance of defect in virtue rather than of viciousness.

But the newer approach to Samuel Wesley does not minimize his faults, which are as open and apparent as his virtues. It arises rather from a fresh understanding of his immense importance in shaping the lives of his sons and therefore in determining the future of Methodism.

First of all there is a new realization that the ties between the father and his sons were exceptionally close. This did not depend upon the excellent education he helped to provide for them, but was due to the intimate interest he took in their development from earliest boyhood. His letters show an equal interest in their studies and their other interests, and it is fascinating to see how with changing years the father is ready both to offer and to seek advice, to be both counsellor and friend. At critical periods in their lives he was at hand to encourage. Thus at Oxford, when they were continually subjected to misrepresentation and ridicule, he wrote concerning their mode of life *'valde probo'*, and then continued: 'Go on in God's Name in the path to which the Saviour directed you and that track therein your father has gone before you. For when I was an undergraduate at Oxford I visited those in the Castle there and reflect on it with great satisfaction to this day.' It was because the sons admired their father's ample scholarship and his disciplined way of life that they were strongly influenced by him in four main directions.

He gave them a love of books and sound learning. During their days at school and in the University they carried the memory of the Epworth study and their father's constant preoccupation either with the reading or writing of books. His own love of Greek and Latin helped them to become exact classical scholars, and the linguistic ability which caused the Rector in his *Dissertations on Job* to collate the Hebrew text with the Chaldee paraphrase and the Septuagint, and to compare versions in Syriac, Arabic, and Latin, caused all three sons to be as interested in the structure of language as in its expression. Almost as a matter of course he could ask John 'to fall to work and read diligently the Hebrew text in the Polyglot and collate it exactly with the Vulgate, writing all, even the least, variations or differences between them'.

It is not to be overlooked that Samuel was a hymn-writer and poet—to be remembered, not for his long effusion on *The Life of Christ* or his *History of the Old and New Testaments* in verse (three volumes), but for his fine hymn on the death of Christ: 'Behold the Saviour of mankind.' His poetic talent was multiplied in all three sons. John was an incomparable translator of hymns, chiefly from German pietism; Charles was, and remains, the greatest hymn-writer on the great evangelical themes of the Gospel; and Samuel junior, as the enquiring may discover in his *Poems on Several Occasions* (London 1862), was a genuine minor poet especially skilled in satire and epigram.

Whilst Samuel was still a boy of sixteen years, the Rector suggested that he might find pleasure and profit in 'translating portions of the Bible into verse'; but as a hymn-writer he was inferior to his brothers, though his hymns beginning 'The Lord of Sabbath let us praise' and 'The morning flowers display their sweets' are remembered still. Far and away his greatest hymn, however, was, like his father's, concerned with the suffering Saviour, but whilst the Rector gave the death a cosmic setting, 'Hark how he groans! while nature shakes And earth's strong pillars bend', the son essayed a more personal reference:

THE RECTOR OF EPWORTH

For me these pangs His soul assail,
  For me the death is borne,
My sins gave sharpness to the nails
  And pointed every thorn.

The Rector's own lifelong devotional and academic interest lay in the study of the Scriptures, and this passion he also communicated to his sons. Samuel junior gave him constant help in the preparation of the *Dissertations on Job*, and the love and knowledge of the Scriptures possessed by John and Charles are outstanding.

John's published works reveal a New Testament scholar who was not only completely familiar with the original Greek, but was a masterly interpreter of the text. This is best illustrated in his *Notes on the New Testament*. His high conception of his task was shown in the preface. He quoted Luther as saying: 'Divinity is nothing but a grammar of the Holy Ghost. To understand this thoroughly we should observe the emphasis which lies on every word; the holy affections expressed thereby and the tempers shown by every writer.' In accordance with his plan, John Wesley made his notes 'as short and plain as possible', and 'declined to go deep into many difficulties lest the ordinary reader be left behind'. In consequence, the *Notes* are still a living and inspiring commentary on the sacred text, and hundreds of the translated words and phrases anticipate the work of the scholars who made the Revised Version.

Charles Wesley's hymns are strongly scriptural, and have delighted those generations who have been brought up on the Bible as an indispensable handbook to living. They have detected echoes of Holy Writ in almost every line, and even so have had to admit that they have not succeeded in tracking all his references to their sources. A writer who could call on Old and New Testaments even within the compass of a single line, and weave so many different threads of Scripture within the texture of a single verse, was one whose facility of pen was only equalled by ripe biblical scholarship.

The second way in which the Rector influenced his sons was by giving them a sturdy orthodoxy with a strong evangelical emphasis. In an age which had tired of religious controversies and had emptied Calvinism of its spiritual content, nothing was left but God as the First Cause, the unmoved mover, infinitely separated from His creatures. Revelation could not light up the chasm, and all that remained was the cold light of reason to illumine man's unaided way.

The two best-known books in the spate of Deistic writings were John Toland's *Christianity not Mysterious*, in which the author left no room for the miraculous and supernatural, and Nicholas Tindal's *Christianity as Old as the Creation*, whose contents are sufficiently indicated by the sub-title, 'The Gospel —a Republication of the Religion of Nature'. The danger of this philosophy was in its making unnecessary the atoning work, miracles, and person of Jesus Christ. The use of reason as the sole determining guide left no place for prayer to God as Father nor for the experience of Him as Saviour and Lord.

Samuel was not a theologian, but he saw acutely where the danger of this rationalistic approach to Christianity lay. It would make revealed religion not only unnecessary, but false. A man would be deprived of both our Lord's divinity and His miracles. As there would be no place for His incarnation, redemptive work, and resurrection, so there would be no credence given to His unique authority in Person and in teaching. The Rector believed that the only proper way to counter this was a firm adherence in sermons and writings to the fundamental tenets of the historic Creeds.

It argues much for his prescience that he realized that rationalism resting only on natural religion had no philosophy of a life beyond death with its pains and rewards. The Deists had taken away the 'terror' from religion, but this in plain language was a removing of the fear of God and the sense of present as well as future Judgement. This in turn robbed the Christian Faith both of its restraints and constraints; as Samuel acutely remarked: 'They would like to annihilate hell so that they might be tolerably happy, more quietly rake through the world, and then sink into nothingness.' Samuel believed that in so desperate an encounter for truth the privates had as much a part to play as the generals, and in particular they were neither to quit their posts nor to cease to give the alarm.

It was in the central citadel of the Faith that Samuel Wesley remained most staunch. He would not tolerate for a moment any compromise over the Lord's divinity. Even though Unitarians only made a moment's difference between the existence of Father and Son, he remained unimpressed. They still think, he said, of a created God and of one subordinate to the Father.

When Susanna was attracted as a young woman to Socinianism,[1] it was her fiancé who by patient argument dissuaded her, and afterwards she confessed that it had been one of life's crowning mercies to have been married to a religious orthodox man and by him to have been 'drawn off from the Socinian heresy'.

After a close study of Samuel Wesley's answers in the *Athenian Oracle* and his *Notes on the Life of Christ*, Luke Tyerman asserted that no follower of John Wesley held the doctrine of Justification by Faith more firmly or clearly than John Wesley's own father.

[1] This term, derived from the theologians Laelius Socinus and Faustus Socinus, indicates a lack of belief in the Trinity, and in the divinity and saving work of Christ.

THE RECTOR OF EPWORTH

This indeed was a dominant note in his preaching. He spoke continually to his parishioners on the saving work of Christ, and he firmly accepted the Arminian and not the Calvinistic view of redemption. He confessed himself unable to believe that there was an election of a determinate number and a reprobation of the rest of mankind. In a notable sentence foreshadowing the later Methodist teaching, he said: 'God has offered the pardon of all sin and the right to life in Christ to all men without exception, on condition of believing and acceptance. Saving faith is a steady belief in Jesus as the Saviour of the world and that He will save me, if I depend on Him and obey His commands.'

Free Churchmen are inclined to swallow hard when they hear that Samuel rejoiced because there were no dissenters in his parish. But in his day dissenting bodies, especially Presbyterian and Congregational Churches, were so infected with Unitarianism that the Rector looked upon dissent as a zealous gardener would look upon weeds in a garden.

It is entirely appropriate that on his very death-bed he should not only prophesy the revival of pure religion, but express his firm conviction that the inward witness was 'the strongest proof of Christianity'. In his teaching on Assurance John was surely influenced by his father's own declared belief in this doctrine.

Had the sons been brought up in one of the

numberless vicarages in which the proclamation of evangelical truth was discounted, they might easily have succumbed to the prevailing rationalism, and in that case the Methodist Revival would never have begun. But none of Samuel's children wavered in the orthodox acceptance of the Christian religion. Surely the main reason for this uncompromising refusal to join in the current intellectual fashion was the example of a father who rejoiced in his Trinitarian faith.

A third formative influence of the father on the sons was in his love of the Anglican Church and more especially of its liturgy and its sacraments. Like every convert, he brought a warm and even passionate love to the Church of his adoption. His distaste and even dislike of dissent was based partly on its suspected republicanism and its defective soteriology, but even more in its separation from the State; the conception of the gathered Church had no attraction for one who coupled love for King and Constitution with love of God and the Church. Samuel was specially interested in Church music. He could not tolerate the paraphrases of Psalms by Sternhold and Hopkins, though he was forced to make use of them. Writing to his son Sammy, he urged him to understand cathedral music, for, he said, he would find Church music a great help to devotion.

Incidentally, the Rector's regard for Church music was fully shared by his sons. John published five musical works, consisting chiefly of psalm- and hymn-tunes. He also wrote some *Directions for Congregational Singing* in which he asked the congregation to sing all, to sing lustily, to sing modestly (no bawling), to sing in time and to sing spiritually; his father would have approved strongly each injunction.

Charles Wesley had a like understanding of the importance of music. In his *Apology for the Enemies to Music* he speaks of its 'sacred powers' and in a short hymn on 1 Samuel 16^{23} he writes:

> *Music, as first by heaven designed*
> *To calm the tumult of the mind,*
> *Relieves us by its sacred aid,*
> *As Saul was well when David play'd.*

It is only a musician with an ear for rhyme and melody who could employ so many metres. Handel and Charles Wesley were on terms of mutual respect, and Charles could write:

> *When Handel strikes the warbling strings,*
> *And plausive angels clap their wings.*

Handel set three of Charles Wesley's hymns to music, and another friend, John Frederick Lampe, a bassoonist in Mr Rich's London Theatre, composed tunes for twenty-four hymns. Samuel Wesley junior said of his father that he played a little German flute at Oxford and was extremely fond of music in his early life, being especially partial to the old masters. He said of Charles that if there were repetitions in a piece of music he knew exactly what part was to be played or sung, and when any failed to give them he would say: 'You have cheated me of a repeat.' He said further that Charles could join in a hymn or simple melody 'tolerably well in tune'. If Charles had possessed no love of music he would not so readily have allowed his two musically gifted sons to give a series of concerts for many years at his London house in Chesterfield Street. Many distinguished people of the day, including the Bishop of London, and Lords Mornington, Dartmouth, Barrington, and De Spencer, were regular subscribers; and so, if only through his sons, Charles moved to some degree in a fashionable circle devoted to music.

But the greatest delight of the Rector was in the sacraments of the Church. In an age in which the Bishop of Oxford (later Archbishop Secker) could recommend his clergy to have at least one celebration between Whitsuntide and Christmas, and in which in great numbers of parish churches the Holy Communion was only administered three times a year, the Rector of Epworth far more frequently observed the sacred rite and dwelt repeatedly on its significance. Indeed, one of his better-known writings is entitled *The Pious Communicant Rightly Prepared, or a discourse concerning the Blessed Sacrament wherein its nature is described, our obligation to frequent communion enforced, and directions given for due preparation of it, behaviour at it and after it, and profiting by it. With prayers and hymns suited to the several parts of that Holy Office. To which is added 'A Short Discourse on Baptism'.* The actual book was not so weighty as its lengthy title might suggest, but he carefully distinguished between the Roman Catholic and Anglican interpretations of Communion and pressed for its frequent observance.

In July 1731 the Rector had a terrible fall from the horse and wagon. He never fully recovered from it, and yet on the following Sunday, although he was in great pain, he not only preached twice, but, according to a letter of Susanna, he 'gave the Sacrament which was too much for him to do but nobody could dissuade him from it'.

It is fitting that when he came to die he should say to his family: 'Tomorrow I will see you all with me round this table that we may drink once more the cup of blessing before we drink it new in the Kingdom of God. With desire have I desired to eat this passover with you before I die.' On the following day he was so weak that only with extreme difficulty could he receive the elements, but Charles noticed that upon receiving the bread and wine he was 'full of faith and peace'.

His love of the Church is best confirmed by the fact that for almost forty years he was a faithful parish priest, strictly observing the discipline of

SONS TO SAMUEL

the Church of England, diligently visiting his parishioners, and offering before them the example of a godly and quiet life. Despite the early suspicion and antagonism of his parishioners, he won their respect and confidence, and in a letter to Samuel junior (28th February 1733) he could say thankfully that after his long labours among them his people 'grew better'. When John Wesley preached on his father's tombstone in 1742, he thought of his father's devoted ministry at Epworth and commented: 'Let none think his labour of love is lost because the fruit does not immediately appear.' The seed sown, he said, had now sprung up, bringing forth 'repentance and remission of sins'.

So powerful an example of filial piety to mother Church must have greatly influenced the three sons. Certainly they all showed more than ordinary devotion to the Anglican Church. In this, John is perhaps the most interesting of the three. His followers now form one of the largest and most influential Churches in Christendom, and long before he died his own actions had made separation from the Church of England inevitable; nevertheless, because of his deep-rooted reverence for the Church of England, he became, ecclesiastically speaking, a schizophrenic. As a later follower, Dr Beaumont, remarked, he was like a rower whose eyes are on the land whilst every stroke of his oars takes him farther from the shore. All his irregular actions, culminating in the assumption of the episcopal right to ordain, were made to the constant plea that he remained a faithful son of the Church of England. When Charles, who in these matters saw far more clearly than his brother, wrote in broken-hearted protest against the ordinations, John Wesley continued to show mild surprise at his vehemence. 'What are you frighted at?' he wrote in August 1785. 'I no more separate from it now than I did in the year 1758. I submit still (though sometimes with a doubting conscience) to "mitred infidels". I do, indeed, vary from them in some points of doctrine and in some points of discipline— by preaching abroad, for instance, by praying extempore, and by forming societies; but not an hair's breadth farther than I believe to be meet, right, and my bounden duty. I walk still by the same rule I have done for between forty and fifty years. I do nothing rashly. It is not likely I should. The highday of my blood is over.'

We must take full account of all the other factors which kept him perversely loyal to his Church, but we shall never fully comprehend his attitude to it unless we always see, standing in the background, the Rector, the first and formative influence in his life.

The loyalty of Samuel junior and Charles to the Church was always completely unambiguous. It will ever be a matter for speculation whether Samuel junior, if he had lived, would ultimately have joined his brothers in the work of the Revival. Because of his early death, he only saw the movement in its first beginnings, when it was partly disfigured by emotional excesses; moreover, his information was received mainly from Mrs Hutton,[2] who in this regard was a tainted witness. She was prejudiced by the harmful influence she thought John Wesley was exerting over her two sons, and she wanted 'this madness' ended. In Samuel's correspondence with John he accepted Mrs Hutton's viewpoint, and, despite the moderation of John's replies, he still believed that the new teaching, especially the doctrine of Assurance, was not consonant with Anglican belief. It is true that in his last letter, written two months before his death, he expressed his joy on hearing of the building of a Charity School, and he wanted a church to be built for the Kingswood colliers. Nevertheless, he was still perturbed by Whitefield's[3] ecclesiastical irregularities and in dread that John might follow in his wake. He did not fear, he said, with the small amount of discipline existing, that the Church would excommunicate John, but that John might excommunicate the Church. This was prescience indeed! Samuel junior, as a High Churchman, Tory, and indeed Jacobite,

[2] Both John and Charles Wesley had lodged with Mrs Hutton on their return from Georgia.
[3] George Whitefield first knew the Wesleys when he became a member of the Holy Club at Oxford. It was on his instigation that John first preached in the open air at Bristol, and despite their doctrinal differences they remained friends until Whitefield's death.

was the last man to cavil at his father's devoted churchmanship.

Charles suffered an incessant tug-of-war between his loyalty to the Methodist Societies, and his brother in particular, and an unswerving devotion to the Church. Whenever the two came into open and unavoidable conflict, it was the Anglican cause that he espoused; but the calmer, more phlegmatic John never really understood how much these struggles told on Charles and even hastened his end.

All three brothers accepted their father's advice to dwell lovingly on the Christian Sacraments and be frequent at Holy Communion. In a remarkable article (*London Quarterly Review*, July 1923) the late Rev. T. H. Barratt showed that Wesley in one year communicated at least once every four days, and in another only a little less.

John republished his early Oxford sermon on 'Constant Communion' (1732) as late as 1788, and said he had no reason to change his view that Communion should be not only frequent, but constant. It is interesting to note that in his *Popery Calmly Considered* he took precisely the same stand as his father against any theory of transubstantiation and the denial of the cup to the laity.

When Charles ceased to itinerate he only gave himself more frequently to the celebration of the Sacrament of the Lord's Supper for the people called Methodists.

SONS TO SAMUEL

It will not be disputed that the three brothers would have been convinced members of the Church of England by training and inclination, but their outstanding zeal owed much to their father's teaching and example.

In the fourth and last place, the Rector shared with his sons his own large vision of the world-wide Church and communicated his own missionary enthusiasm.

The cruel might suggest that when the young Rector of Epworth offered himself as a missionary to the Society for the Propagation of the Gospel he was only anxious to escape from the all-too-cramping limitations of a remote Lincolnshire parish. But criticism is confounded when it is remembered that at the very end of his life his missionary enthusiasm was still unabated. His active support of Oglethorpe's scheme for colonizing Georgia was kindled by the thought of setting forth the Christian witness among the American Indians. We know this, because he said that had he been younger he would have learnt the language in order to teach the natives, but that as it was, he was willing to let his curate go in his place. His one great hymn combines in dramatic fashion the cosmic and personal aspects of Christ's redeeming work. Charles Wesley, in his emphasis upon God's saving love for the world and for one lost sinner, did not sharpen the antithesis more perfectly than Samuel in the opening verse of the hymn—

THE RECTOR OF EPWORTH

Behold the Saviour of mankind,
Nailed to the shameful tree!
How vast the love that Him inclined
To bleed and die for thee!

If the first line speaks of all men, the last line brings each separate sinner within the empire of so vast a love. This is a missionary emphasis caught up and developed by his sons; through them the world was to be made familiar with the conception of One who died for all and therefore died for each. The lesson, however, was learnt from a father who from an Epworth Rectory could look upon the world as a parish where God might be served.

Any fresh estimate of Methodist beginnings will not touch the status of Susanna, but it will recognize the powerful influence of the Rector upon the thinking and practice of his sons. Let him keep all his blemishes; he still remains the first great fashioner of the Methodist story.

CHAPTER TWO

The Three Brothers

ANY FRESH look at Methodist beginnings must result in a more assured place for Samuel junior, the eldest of the Epworth family. He is important in his own right, for it is he undoubtedly who supported the family during the most trying financial period at Epworth, when the brood received constant additions, and the Rector had not only to support the household, but provide for his children's education, especially that of John and Charles. Samuel's own education began at Westminster School in 1704, and when in 1707 he became a King's Scholar the financial burden on his parents was lifted. In 1711 he entered Christ Church, Oxford, and even before he took his degree was known as a scholar and a wit. Returning to Westminster as an Usher (assistant master), he immediately set himself to repair the family's fortunes. It was said reliably that he divided his income between himself and his parents and family, but forbade any mention of it during his lifetime.

Samuel lived sufficiently long for it to be obvious that he had neither the handsome appearance nor the outstanding gifts of his two brothers. He spoke of himself in a letter as hoarse in speech and short-sighted in vision, and his gifts were displayed not in the pulpit, but at the teaching desk. It seems tolerably certain that if he had not persisted in his Jacobitism and more particularly in his devotion to the banished Bishop Atterbury, he might have succeeded to the Vice-Headmastership of Westminster School; as it was, he became Headmaster of Tiverton Grammar School in 1732, and in seven years greatly increased the numbers attending and the reputation of the school in the county.

As a writer of short satiric verse he had few equals in his day; but, unlike Swift or Dryden, he was too poor a hater for his darts to be envenomed, and even his particular target of attack, Sir Robert Walpole, was apostrophized as 'Bob' whilst his policies were being attacked. In a few lyrics, elegies, and epigrams, he is worthy of inclusion in any anthology of eighteenth-century poetry, but John's remarkable understatement of Charles's powers could more fittingly be applied to Samuel. He had 'a talent for poetry'; light was given him, but fire was denied.

The importance of Samuel for the Wesley saga lies in his extraordinary influence over both John and Charles. John went to Charterhouse in 1714 whilst still a few months short of eleven years of age, and when Samuel returned from Oxford the following year the brothers were not widely separated. At the end of the school year John must often have made his home with his elder brother. He entered the same Oxford College, taking the same classical studies, and in at least one letter declared that apart from seeing his mother the one thing he most desired was to see Westminster again. He had heard of Samuel's broken leg, and quoted from the *Spectator* (No. 574) the story of the sailor who fell from the mainmast, breaking a leg, and gave thanks that he had not broken his neck.

His indebtedness to his elder brother both in financial and brotherly counsel was reflected in the letter he wrote immediately upon his election to a Fellowship at Lincoln College, Oxford. He returned 'sincere and hearty thanks as well for your past kindness as for the fresh instance you now give me, in the pains you take to qualify me for the enjoyment of that success which I owe chiefly, not to say, wholly, to your interest'. In his Oxford letters to Samuel, John used to send verse translations he had composed from Latin poets, particularly from the *Odes* of Horace. He also sent a vigorous paraphrase of the forty-sixth Psalm, which concluded—

> *Let war's devouring surges rise*
> *And rage on every side,*
> *The Lord of Hosts our refuge is*
> *And Jacob's God our guide.*

One of the longest letters to his brother was written from Lincoln College (6th December 1726) and showed how Hetty Wesley's clandestine elopement with her faithless suitor had involved the whole family in an angry quarrel. To his great credit, John had not shared 'the inconceivable exasperation' of his father against Hetty, but had chosen rather to preach in Wroot Church against rash judging.[4] His father had been hurt, and news of the offence reached Samuel, who thought his parents' feelings had been too lightly regarded. John's defence of his action was based not only on his belief in the 'charity due to injured persons', but on a strong disapproval of Samuel's willingness to hear one side of the story only. Later, Samuel came substantially to John's point of view, but this letter shows that John was never ready to accept either reproof or advice from his elder brother unless he was persuaded they were justified.

In a letter written on 17th November 1731, John defends himself against certain requirements in manner and deportment which Samuel thought to be necessary for a clergyman and which John maintained were questions of temperament and disposition. Strangely, the John Wesley who later on was to be known for his continual cheerfulness now asked: 'Mirth, I grant, is fit for you, but does it follow that it is fit for me?'

A larger field of disagreement was in John Wesley's steadfast refusal to follow his father as Rector of

---

[4] Wroot Church, 28th August 1726, on 'Universal Charity, or the charity due to wicked persons'.

Epworth even though Samuel staunchly supported the Rector in making this appeal to John. Samuel strove to secure John's acceptance of the Epworth living by laying down the principle (8th February 1735) that 'the *order of the Church* stakes you down and the more you struggle, you will be held the faster'; but he forgot that his brother was a master of logic. John answered his arguments one by one, and concluded that Samuel implied that the priest who does not undertake the first parochial living that is offered is perjured. As well argue, said John, that the tutor who, being in orders, never takes a parish is perjured. This, of course, was precisely the position of Samuel, who, being a priest, had still remained a schoolmaster. Samuel must have been checked, but he was not overwhelmed, and after he had returned once more to the attack, John had to reply in a final letter on the subject that he had all reasonable evidence that as a clergyman he could serve God better in his present station than anywhere else.

The third and last argument between the brothers was the most serious and vital of all. It came to no conclusion, because in the midst of the correspondence Samuel suddenly fell ill and died. The controversy well illustrates both the unflinching loyalty of the High Churchman, Samuel, to all the rubrics of the established Church, and the equal determination of John not to allow his brother's disparaging criticism to deflect him one inch from his chosen way.

THE THREE BROTHERS

Samuel knew his brother, and feared his strength even whilst he deplored the Church's weakness. He had no dread of what the Church might do to John, but only what John might do to the Church, and in the event he proved to be right. Considering his long series of irregular acts, John was treated with surprising tolerance by the Church, and it was by his own action and not through ecclesiastical procedure that he made it impossible for Methodism to be a society within the mother Church.

A number of the letters which passed between the Wesley brothers were concerned not with order but with doctrine. The elder brother could not tolerate the new emphasis on the witness of the Spirit, which he found to be vain and delusory; and indeed in those first days the excitable demeanour of converts and the insistence upon 'assurance' must have set the doctrine in a most unfavourable light. John, however, meant by assurance not the transitory feelings of the more emotional, but the experience of a new standing in Christ in which the believer's confidence depends upon Christ's objective work. 'I build on Christ, the Rock of Ages; on His sure mercies described in His Word; and on His promises, all which I know are yea and amen' (30th October 1738). This particular letter made such an impression that John in a later epistle was able to rejoice at 'the mildness and love' in his brother's heart and the new temper in which he was conducting the argument. Nevertheless, Samuel was not satisfied and John spoke in a final letter of what he had found. 'Saw you him that was a lion till then and is now a lamb; him that was a drunkard, but now exemplarily sober; the whoremonger that was, who now abhors the very lusts of the flesh?' In time Sammy might have been convinced that the new movement had no theological extravagances, but nothing would have reconciled him to the building of preaching-houses, the appointment of assistant preachers, and the formation of circuits. This was hidden from his eyes, but he had sufficient insight to know his brother's authority and to be disquieted by the shape of things to come.

A final summary of the relation between the two brothers must rest on the fact that none of their differences could persuade the one to yield to the other. To the very end John could sign himself 'Yours and my sister's most affectionate brother', and yet quietly and steadfastly continue in his own way and in his own opinions. Samuel could admire and love his brother but remain unsatisfied with his views and ecclesiastical behaviour. This perhaps is not astonishing, since he was thirteen years the older man, and so for half his life John had been to him a mere stripling; the marvel is that John should have grown so rapidly to a position in which he freely argued on equal terms with his elder brother as though they were equal in age and status.

THE THREE BROTHERS

The relationship between Charles and Samuel was emphatically never of that kind. That was partly because the gulf of years was even wider; when a man is seventeen years older than you are, it is difficult even in adult life to forget the seniority. Even more significant, however, was the fact that when still only nine years of age Charles was sent to Westminster to be under his brother's care. This ensured for Charles the best classical education of the day, because not only did he attend for ten years one of the better schools in the country, but his brother remained an unofficial guide and tutor. Through his oversight, Charles, after five years at Westminster, became a King's Scholar, and his expenses thereafter were borne by the School.

Charles Wesley was the least ambitious of men; by temperament, equipment, and desire, he was content to follow, provided he approved the leader. Consequently, both at school and in his undergraduate days, he showed an almost filial respect and affection for Samuel. As he absorbed his teaching, so equally he accepted his High Churchmanship. Then came an almost abrupt change of dominant loyalty, for when John returned to Oxford as Fellow of Lincoln College, Charles transferred the headship of the Holy Club to him without the slightest struggle. Some warning of this change in Charles can be detected in a letter he wrote to John early in 1729. He told his brother that he had awakened from his lethargy shortly after John had left Oxford to become his father's curate at Wroot. He continued: 'It is through your means I firmly believe that God will accomplish what he began in me.' Indeed, he went farther still: 'I would willingly write a Diary of my actions but do not know how to go about it. What particulars am I to take notice of? . . . I am to mark all the good and ill I do, and what beside? . . . If you would direct me to the same or like method to your own, I would gladly follow it; for I am fully convinced of the usefulness of such an undertaking. I shall be at a stand-still till I hear from you.'

When John came back to Oxford as Fellow and Tutor, he found that Charles had started the Holy Club and with a small group of like-minded students had given himself to devotional exercises and serious Bible study. Straightway John took over what Charles had begun and developed it in his own fashion. The company agreed to spend some evenings of each week together. On week evenings, in addition to the Greek New Testament, they read in company certain classics, but on a Sunday evening they read some book of divinity; they also accepted a searching system of self-examination. This inward culture of the soul was counter-balanced by social and philanthropic work in the city of Oxford.

It was John who drew up the rules for the company and arranged for the conduct of the meetings. When Charles went to stay with his brother Samuel in 1729 it was already obvious to the older man that John had now the ruling word. He noted not only the lack of Charles's former hearty appetite, but also a new seriousness, and commented somewhat ambiguously that he had grown extremely like his brother. When Charles wrote to John of this summer visit, he refused to characterize the entertainment offered, but he did say that in the remote possibility of his ever being disposed to disagree with John, the one factor which would prevent it would be 'somebody's indignation that we agree so well'. Evidently both Samuel and his wife had commented with some acerbity on John's hold over his brother.

This was soon to be illustrated in the most convincing manner. John did not go to Georgia because he had the slightest personal desire to leave the studious cloistered life of Oxford. Had he not declined the Epworth living, giving twenty-six reasons for his refusal? He had good reason for going, however, for he believed that the experience of Georgia might give him the chance to save his own soul, and the fact that he shrank from it, as well as from separation from his mother, only made the call more imperative. Charles had no reason for going except that his brother wished it. Samuel realized this, and wrote in the strongest terms to Charles urging him against the decision. Nevertheless, he had to acknowledge defeat: 'Jack knew his strength and used it. His will was strong enough to bend you to go, though not me to consent. I freely own 'twas the will of Jack but am not yet convinced 'twas the will of God.'

Most certainly it was not the will of Charles, for as he later confessed, his only thought was of spending all his days at Oxford, and neither the prospect of being secretary to General Oglethorpe nor of taking Holy Orders made the slightest appeal to him. Nevertheless, for John's sake he became both secretary and clergyman. His inner state of mind was only disclosed in a letter written towards the very end of his life: 'My brother who always had the ascendant over me persuaded me to accompany him and Mr Oglethorpe to Georgia. I exceedingly dreaded entering into Holy Orders but he overruled me here also, and I was ordained deacon by the Bishop of Oxford, and the next Sunday, priest by the Bishop of London.'

Seventeen days before his death, Samuel recognized once again that, despite his own expressed misgivings, his brother Charles was unalterably associated with John in the first stages of the Revival. In a letter to his mother he wrote: 'It was with exceeding concern and grief I heard you had countenanced a spreading delusion so far as to be one of Jack's congregation. Is it not enough that I am bereft of both my brothers, but must my mother follow too?'

When he died, therefore, he might reasonably have supposed that his hold over Charles had been finally lost and that John was now completely master both of the convictions and affections of his younger brother. But the dead Samuel still had a greater hold over Charles than John could ever credit. Indeed, the career of Charles might be epitomized as a tug-of-war in which at one time he was securely held by brother Samuel, then as completely held by John, and, finally, after a long tussle between the dead and living masters of his life, came at life's close once more under the dominance of his eldest brother. This was due in part to the lifelong authority that those exert who fashion our thinking in childhood and youth, but also to John's bold and irregular ecclesiastical course in the prosecution of his mission.

When to John's pamphlet, *Reasons Against a Separation from the Church of England* (1758), seven hymns were added, the united weight of the brothers seemed sufficient to make any separation impossible; but John was willing to take account of circumstances and the needs of the work in a way Charles could not. So when, on the authority of Lord King and Bishop Stillingfleet, John regarded himself in the New Testament sense as a bishop, he was ready to ordain men to minister to the colonists, so rudely deprived of shepherds by the War of American Independence. It was a classic illustration of Charles's own dictum that my brother's first object was the Methodists and then the Church. 'Mine was first the Church and then the Methodists.'

The vehemence of Charles's letter to a clergyman (28th April 1785) can only be explained by the tenacious hold of the Anglican Church over one who, although he never parted from John in evangelical doctrine and witness, shared increasingly in old age his brother Samuel's dread of ecclesiastical innovations. Concerning John's ordinations he wrote: 'My brother does not and will not see that he has renounced the principles and practice of his whole life, that he has acted contrary to all his declarations, protestations and writings; robbed his friends of their boasting; and left an indelible blot on his name, as long as it shall be remembered! Thus our partnership here is dissolved but not our friendship.' This was the stand which, on the same grounds and with the same mixture of indignation and grief, Samuel would have taken.

The conclusion must be that the brothers Samuel and John Wesley were men of strong character and convictions who were never able to change each other's point of view. This constantly irked Samuel, who, being many years the senior, could not lightly accept that growing spiritual and intellectual independence of John which made him go his own way in refusing the Epworth living, offering himself for Georgia, and committing himself to field preaching.

There are, nevertheless, those who see in the last days of the elder brother an indication that he had begun to accept the new Methodist movement. They are strengthened in that presumption by the powerful support of John Wesley himself. In his *Journal* he wrote: 'We could not but rejoice at hearing from one who had attended my brother in all his weakness, that several days before he went hence, God had given him a calm and full assurance of his interest in Christ. Oh! may everyone who opposes it be thus convinced that this doctrine is of God.' In this interpretation of his brother's ease of spirit, however, John undoubtedly argued beyond the merits of the evidence. Southey was surely right when he said that Samuel's state of mind had nothing to do with the doctrine of assurance then being preached by his brothers, but was 'the sure and certain hope of a sincere and humble Christian who trusted in the merits of his Saviour and the mercy of his God'. There is no question that had Samuel lived he would have continued as a critic, albeit friendly, of a movement whose methods he so much disliked.

Charles, at the end of his days, recaptured the mood and very tones of Samuel, and in despair urged John to caution, reconsideration and retreat. But if John was unwilling to listen at the start, he was certainly unwilling to listen at the close. Once it had been Charles and himself against the elder brother, and now it was he who stood alone against Charles and Samuel's ghost. But the die had been irrevocably cast. At all costs the work of saving souls in the new world as well as the old must go on. The colonists in America must hear the word and receive the Sacraments, and therefore ordained men must be sent to them. Even Charles with the hand of a dead brother upon him must not hinder. 'If you will go hand-in-hand with me, do. But do not hinder if you will not help. However, with or without help, I creep on.' Brother Samuel, speaking once more through the anxious tones of Charles, was strong, but he was not strong enough; he belonged to the old world, and a new one was calling.

CHAPTER THREE

The Unalienable Friends

THE TITLE of this chapter will not seem appropriate to those who remember the stormy interference of Charles in the proposal of John to make Grace Murray his wife; neither will it seem fitting to those who recall John's disappointment when the happily married Charles decided to settle down in Bristol and leave the ceaseless itinerary to his brother. Even more disturbing to the critical is the difference between the brothers in the matter of Methodist polity, a difference which increased as time wore on. The sore thrust of that divergence was felt for thirty years.

Relations between Methodism and the Church of England were not easy. Charles himself had been denied the sacrament of the Temple Church in Bristol in 1741, and that rude rejection often befell both preachers and laymen. But a more serious difficulty was that a number of the clergy were men of dissolute character. The view of many Methodists was forcibly expressed by Joseph Cownley, one of the best and most eloquent Methodist preachers. He set out the reasons why he would not hear drunkards preach or read prayers, and John Wesley confessed:

'I cannot answer his reasons.' His views were fully shared by the ardent Thomas Walsh as well as by Charles and Edward Perronet, the Methodist sons of the Vicar of Shoreham.

Charles regarded this rising tide of discontent with apprehension, and opened his heart (1754) in a long epistle to the Rev. Walter Sellon, a former master at Kingswood School. Sellon wrote at once to John Wesley and to Charles Perronet, though evidently without result, for he was urged by Charles to return to the attack: 'Write again and spare not. My brother took no notice to me of your letter. Since the Melchizedekians have been taken in, I have been excluded from his Cabinet Council. They know me too well to trust him with me. He is come so far as to believe separation quite lawful only not yet expedient. They are indefatigable in urging him to go so far that he may not be able to retreat. He may lay on hands, they say, without separating.' Then came the full disclosure of Charles's mind: 'In May our Conference is. You must be there, if alive. We can hold it no longer (the Methodist preachers I mean) but quickly divide to the right or left, the Church or the Meeting.' Church or Meeting—that was the issue for Charles; either Methodists must conform loyally to the usages of the Church of England or become Dissenters. He would have forced the issue on every preacher, for on 5th February 1755 he wrote: 'We must know the heart of every preacher and give them their choice of the Church or the Meeting. The wound can no longer be healed slightly. Those who are disposed to separate had best do it while we are yet alive.'

The Conference of 1755 met in Leeds, and on 6th May both the brothers spoke vigorously on the issue of separation before the sixty-three preachers assembled there. On the third day of the debate all were seemingly agreed that, whether separation was or was not lawful, it was not expedient. Charles felt it to be a doubtful victory, but he realized quite rightly that many were silent but not satisfied. While his feelings were still warm from the Conference and the stimulus of the debate, Charles wrote an eloquent rhymed epistle on the Church of England to his brother, and four thousand copies were quickly sold. It ends with a famous plea—

> *Partner of my reproach, who justly claim*
> *The larger portion of the glorious shame,*
> *My pattern in the work and cause Divine,*
> *Say is thy heart as* bigoted *as mine?*
> *Wilt thou with me in the old Church remain,*
> *And share her weal or woe, her loss, her gain,*
> *Spend in her service thy last drop of blood,*
> *And die—to build the temple of our God!*
>
> .   .   .
>
> *Was it our aim disciples to collect,*
> *To raise a party, or to found a sect!*

SONS TO SAMUEL

No; but to spread the power of Jesus' name,
Repair the walls of our Jerusalem,
Revive the piety of ancient days,
And fill the earth with our Redeemer's praise.[1]

John Wesley quite honestly could not understand what all this excessive pother was about. He pointed out to his brother that the preachers (except the ordained) had promised 'not to administer the sacrament nor to separate from the Church', and he added somewhat pathetically: 'Here is Charles Perronet raving because his friends have given up all, and Charles Wesley because they have given up nothing; and I, in the midst, staring and wondering both at one and the other.' Once again in the Conference of 1756 the brothers made a joint declaration never to separate from the Church, but Charles was still filled with misgivings. When in 1758 John Wesley published his *Twelve Reasons Against Separating from the Church of England*, Charles added a personal note: 'I subscribe to the twelve reasons of my brother with all my heart—I am quite clear it is neither expedient nor lawful for me to separate, and I never had the least inclination or temptation to do so. My affection for the Church is as strong as ever, and I clearly see my calling which is to live and die in her communion. Would to God that all the Methodist preachers were in this respect like-minded with Charles Wesley.'

[1] *The Poetical Works of John and Charles Wesley* (1870 Edn), VI.62-3.

THE UNALIENABLE FRIENDS

At the close of 1779 occurred a gesture of defiance to Wesley's rule which alarmed Charles afresh. At the Conference of that year a certain Mr McNab had been appointed to the Bath Circuit, but when an Irish clergyman known to Wesley stayed in Bath, John Wesley gave him permission to preach every Sunday evening in the Methodist Chapel whilst he was there. This offended Mr McNab, who claimed that he had been sent there by Conference rather than by Wesley, and that he intended to preach. John recorded in his *Journal* for 22nd November that together with his brother he set out for Bath and found 'the society was torn in pieces and thrown into utmost confusion'. On the next day he read the society a paper in which he observed that 'the rules of our preachers were fixed by me before any Conference existed'. In particular he cited the twelfth rule: 'Above all, you are to preach when and where I appoint.' In the upshot, at a meeting of the preachers, McNab was expelled. But as Christopher Hopper observed in a letter to his friend Joseph Cownley: 'McNab is a true Highlander and would make a very good chieftain. He is too high blood.' Such a man was not lightly to be suppressed, and because of the ensuing agitation John Wesley received him back again as preacher at the Conference of 1780.

Charles, who had been delighted by John's strong exercise of authority a few months earlier, was now in despair at what he considered to be a weak surrender to the preachers. His underlying dread that they might over-rule John in his declining years showed itself in a sharp letter: 'I can do no good. I can prevent no evil. You know I cannot command my temper and you have not courage to stand by me. . . . I am not sure they will not prevail upon you to ordain them. You claim the power, only say it is not probable you shall exercise it. I want better security.' In his despair he wrote:

> *Why should I longer now contend*
> *My last important moments spend*
>   *In buffeting the air!*
> *In warning those who will not see,*
> *But rest in blind security*
>   *And rush into the snare!*

It was in 1784 that these fears overwhelmed him. After the War of American Independence, the eighteen thousand Methodists in America were unable to receive the Sacrament because of the lack of those episcopally ordained. John Wesley sought in vain to persuade the Bishop of London to ordain a man or men for America, and when he was refused proceeded himself solemnly to ordain Thomas Coke as Superintendent of the work in America, and gave him authority to set apart Francis Asbury as his co-superintendent. These were in effect episcopal ordinations, as Charles Wesley in his bitterness well realized. He delivered himself in a biting epigram:

> *How easily are bishops made,*
> *By man or woman's whim.*
> *Wesley his hands on Coke hath laid,*
> *But who laid hands on him?*

In a letter to a clergyman named Dr Chandler, he declared that he could scarcely believe that in his eighty-second year his brother, his own intimate friend and companion, should have 'assumed the episcopal character, ordained elders, consecrated a bishop, and sent him to ordain lay preachers in America'.

Then he indulged in a gloomy prognostication of the probable outcome of so rash a step: 'Those poor sheep in the wilderness, the American Methodists, will lose all their influence and importance: they will turn aside to vain janglings: they will settle again upon their lees: and like other sects of Dissenters come to nothing.' This is scarcely the picture of American Methodism today!

He went so far as to tell Dr Chandler that it meant 'the partnership is here dissolved but not the friendship. I have taken him for better for worse till death us do part, or rather, re-unite us in love inseparable. I have lived on earth a little too long who have lived to see this evil day. . . .'

John was fortified not only by arguments he had

accepted from Lord King's *Account of the Primitive Church*, but by the necessity of the ordinations if proper spiritual provision was to be made for the colonists. He tried patiently to meet his brother's many objections. In answer to a letter from Charles in which he had pleaded with John in the light of what he owed to his father, his brother (Samuel) and himself, not to break down the bridge, John wrote one of his best-remembered letters, part of which has already been quoted. It is dated Plymouth Dock, 19th August 1785, and in it he declares: 'I firmly believe I am a scriptural episkopos as much as any man in England or in Europe; for the uninterrupted succession I know to be a fable which no man ever did or can prove. But this does in no wise interfere with my remaining in the Church of England from which I have no more desire to separate than I had fifty years ago.... Perhaps, if you had kept close to me, I might have done better. However with or without help, I creep on. And as I have hitherto, so I trust I shall always be Your affectionate friend, and brother.'

Charles was not convinced by the argument, but responded as always to the appeal of brotherly love: 'I do go on, or rather creep on, in the old way in which we set out together, and trust to continue in it until I finish my course. . . . I thank you for your intention to remain my friend. Herein is my heart as your heart.' And then, in words which echo his sentiments in the earlier letter to Dr Chandler, he concluded: 'Whom God has joined let no man put asunder. . . . We have taken each other for better for worse till death do us part—no, but to unite eternally.'

In that spirit he attended the Conference of 1786 and wrote to a friend during its course: 'My brother and I and the preachers were unanimous for remaining in the old ship.' It was his last Conference, though John and he made several more journeys together, and less than a year before his death he wrote affectionately: 'Stand to your own proposal. Let us agree to differ. I leave America and Scotland to your latest thoughts and recognitions.'

Despite therefore the difference over Grace Murray which caused John such hurt and sorrow, despite John's disappointment over his brother's decision to discontinue active itinerancy, and most of all despite their deep-seated ecclesiastical disagreements, the partnership was never dissolved except by death. It remains the most outstanding example either in secular or religious history of two brothers, each with native genius, whose gifts were complementary and who did a work together which neither could have achieved alone.

The partnership was fashioned at Oxford, in Georgia, and through a like experience of conversion. Then it was tested in the decade of persecution and the work of the Methodist Revival. Thus there are three preparatory phrases to consider in the

SONS TO SAMUEL

alliance of John and Charles Wesley before they proclaimed under an open sky the glad news of universal salvation.

John came up to Charterhouse in 1714—the year in which his elder brother returned from Oxford as Usher at Westminster. Charles Wesley did not enter Westminster School until 1716, but for four years the three Wesley brothers were in London together. During term time John was separated from the other two, but vacations must often have been spent at Samuel's house in Dean's Yard. It was there in 1715 that Samuel had taken his bride, Ursula Berry, 'though gay, religious, and though young, discreet'. There are no stories linking the three brothers in these years, but we know that whilst Samuel was able to give continual help to Charles in his studies he did not neglect any chance of assisting John. In 1719 he wrote to his father: 'My brother Jack, I can faithfully assure you, gives you no manner of discouragement from breeding your third son a scholar.' A little later that year he wrote to his father: 'Jack is with me, and a brave boy, learning Hebrew as fast as he can.'

Yet it was not until Charles Wesley came to Christ Church that he and John were thrown constantly together. It is true that the very year Charles entered Christ Church (1726) John removed from that college to take up his rooms as Fellow of Lincoln, but John's time-table had become more his own, and

THE UNALIENABLE FRIENDS

despite his lectures in Greek and Logic, he had time for outside pursuits.

Not the least of these were his most pleasant visits to Stanton, Buckland, and Broadway under the shadow of the Cotswold Hills. Already, before Charles had come to Oxford, John had travelled on many occasions that forty miles of horse-riding which brought him to the warm buff stone, the rich green, and the gentle hills and dales of the delectable Cotswold country. Perhaps he had only half an eye for their beauties, because in the Stanton Rectory he was entranced by the good breeding, unaffected piety, and genial society of the remarkable Kirkham family. Robert Kirkham, son of the Rector, was the ostensible cause of these visits, but he was wise enough to know that John's fancy had been caught by his younger sister, and he at least desired the friendship to grow. In a letter dated February 1727 he spoke of Sally with her 'inward smiles and signs and abrupt expressions concerning you. . . . I must conclude and subscribe myself, your most affectionate friend, and *brother* I wish I might write.'

It is never wise to speak of John Wesley being in love, because his idealization of all women and his strange, sensitive, fastidious approach to them confirms an impression that he was 'a eunuch for the Kingdom of God's sake'. As the love of God came more and more to possess him, so less and less did he lean upon any man or woman. At this early stage, however, he could dance, enjoy both plays and novels, take his turn in a parlour game, and show an uncommonly good talent in composing light verse. In the company of Betty and Sarah Kirkham, and later of Mrs Pendarves,[2] a young, cultivated and lovely widow, he was completely at ease. The probability is that Charles never came so fully into this romantic idyll in a pastoral setting, but he has his place in the correspondence in which, after the fashion of the times, John became Cyrus, Charles Araspes, Sally Varanese, and Mary Pendarves Aspasia.

The brothers were separated by long intervals when John left Oxford on 24th August 1727, to assist his father at Epworth and Wroot, but at the end of 1729 he returned, and at once the brothers were thrown together in that close partnership which only death dissolved.

The Holy Club was in existence with Charles as head when John resumed his duties as Fellow of Lincoln, but Charles began a lifetime habit of giving place to John. It was inevitable in any case, for as John Gambold, one of the group, confessed: 'Mr John Wesley was always the chief manager for which he was very fit: for he not only had more learning and experience than the rest but he was blest with such activity that he always seemed to be gaining

[2] Later, as Mrs Delaney, she was one of the best-known and admired women of her day, and in her late years enjoyed the close friendship of the Royal Family and had a house near Windsor Castle.

ground, and such steadiness that he lost none. . . .'
At the start the four friends[3] met only on Sunday evenings, but in time they met each evening between 6 and 9 p.m., and after devotions, which included the study of the Greek New Testament, they discussed the work of the day and the plans of the morrow. They fasted on Wednesdays and Fridays, and received the Sacrament once a week.

Their scheme of living made provision for rigid self-examination, private devotion and works of charity. Like the Rector of Epworth before them, they visited both the Jail and Workhouse and gave help to the sick and aged. So prodigal did John seem in the expenditure of time and energy that brother Samuel on a spring visit in 1732 wrote feelingly:

> *Does John seem bent beyond his strength to go*
> *To his frail carcase literally foe,*
> *Lavish of health, as if in haste to die,*
> *And shorten time t'ensure eternity?*

Gradually the Club increased in numbers, and when the Wesleys sailed for Georgia the fourteen members included Benjamin Ingham, who was to accompany them and after a spell in Moravianism to start his own small society,[4] Thomas Broughton, who later became secretary of the Society for

---

[3] Besides the Wesleys, William Morgan and Robert Kirkham were the first members.

[4] The Inghamites could still be found in dwindling numbers in the present century in parts of Lancashire and Yorkshire.

Promoting Christian Knowledge, John Gambold, later a Moravian bishop, James Hervey, who was to attain national fame as a devotional writer, and George Whitefield, who with the Wesleys was a progenitor of the great revival. Always, however, at the heart of the Club's life were the brothers Wesley, and in those years John seemed so effortlessly in ascendancy over Charles that when the younger brother paid a visit to Westminster in 1729 Samuel and his wife were astonished.

Once Charles had consented to accompany his brother, Dr Burton, who had launched the appeal for the new colony and had requested John to go, urged on him the need for ordination. How much better, he said, that Oglethorpe should have two clergymen than one. But Charles had no such intention, and once again it was only the strong intervention of his brother that decided the issue. His sense of unsuitability for the job was entirely justified by events; he proved an unwilling and unsuccessful secretary, and a stiff and inelastic clergyman. Worst of all, he and General Oglethorpe allowed themselves to be duped by the lying tales of two vindictive women and so were estranged from each other. As always, his spiritual distress had physical symptoms, and his dysentery reduced his strength so greatly, that when Ingham went off to Savannah to bring back John, he scarcely expected to find Charles alive on his return.

THE UNALIENABLE FRIENDS

At once John essayed the risky journey of eighty miles down the coast and brought much-needed calm to his brother's troubled spirit. He gave him wise counsel, restored him to Oglethorpe's favour, wrote all his letters, fulfilled his spiritual functions, and only left Frederica when his brother was able fully to resume his duties.

But Oglethorpe was now fully persuaded that Charles had no future in the colony, and four months later sent him back with despatches for the trustees. Charles had no thought of returning, and with his resignation sent a Latin quotation which he translated:

> *Sir to yourself your slighted gifts I leave*
> *Less fit for me to take, than you to give.*

Since the two brothers were separated by so many weary miles in Georgia, and had each his different task, the partnership consisted more in a common assessment of their own inadequacy than in any joint achievements. They had both suffered at the hands of unscrupulous women and unstable friends; they had known physical weakness and mental torment; worst of all, it had seemed that their work had been in vain. Whitefield, however, saw more clearly than John when he landed in Georgia, in May 1738, and recorded in his *Journal:* 'The good Mr John Wesley has done in America is inexpressible. His name is very precious among the people; and he has laid a foundation that I hope neither men or devils will be able to shake. O that I may follow him as he has followed Christ.' John had no glimmer of consciousness of any work well done, and fourteen months after, when he returned to London (3rd February 1738) the brothers were able to lament together the failure in Georgia and the bleak prospect in England.

Charles had been welcomed by many friends and had paid many visits to Oxford, but despite his occupation with many affairs, he was sick in body and restless in mind. His sense of duty compelled him to make plans for his return to the colony, but all his inclinations and the vehement entreaties of his mother pulled him in the opposite direction. John's report on the unsettled, unhappy state of the colony made him feel that here was an added reason for going to the place of greatest need, but by the end of February he became desperately ill and the doctor advised him that the voyage itself would be fatal. Yielding to his brother's good sense, Charles resigned his position as secretary to General Oglethorpe on 3rd April, and so was finally freed for his life work.

The final event which forged their partnership was their evangelical conversion. It is remarkable that both brothers in the same period of time were uncertain of their future, mentally depressed, and unable to find peace with God. At this critical period they both came under the influence of Peter Böhler, a

THE UNALIENABLE FRIENDS

Moravian missionary who had arrived in London on his way to Georgia and South Carolina. Böhler convinced them separately that salvation was an act of faith in God's grace, and was able to convince John that it could take place in a moment of time. This teaching Charles could not accept, but on the day before Böhler left, he declared to him his great hunger for God and his conviction that he would receive the atonement before he died.

Under Moravian influence, both brothers had come, therefore, to a state compounded of restlessness, despair and expectancy. Indeed, like Bunyan's pilgrim they could see yonder a shining light, and like him they kept that light in their eye. They recognized that salvation came by a faith which they did not possess but longed to have, and they knew no rest until that faith became their own.

If Peter Böhler was the main precipitating influence in their conversion, a second factor was a new understanding, under Moravian tutelage, of Luther. In the week preceding his conversion Charles found Luther's *Commentary on the Galatians* to be 'nobly full of faith'. He wrote in his *Journal:* 'Who would believe our Church had been founded on this important article of justification by faith alone? I am astonished I should ever think this a new doctrine. . . .' Charles had received the commentary from a Mr William Holland, who was a well-to-do painter in Basinghall Street, but also both an Anglican and a Moravian 'Congregation Elder'. He listened while Charles read the preface aloud, and when he heard Luther's words, 'What, have we then nothing to do? No, nothing![5] but only accept of Him who of God is made unto us wisdom and righteousness and sanctification and redemption', he felt a great burden falling off and his heart was so filled with peace and love that he burst into tears. John Wesley, in his account of his strangely warmed heart at the Aldersgate Street Meeting-House on 24th May, speaks of a man reading from Luther's *Preface to the Romans*, and it has been persuasively conjectured by Nehemiah Curnock that William Holland was that reader, and that he read not from the *Preface to the Romans*, but from that part of Luther's *Preface to the Galatians* which had brought so great a sense of peace and joy to himself. If that conjecture is right, both brothers were influenced by the same passage from Luther,[6] and as Charles read it to Holland so Holland read it to John. Only the discovery of a missing diary would put the matter beyond dispute. The all-important fact is that for both brothers Luther was a tutor leading them to Christ.

Strangely, the last precipitating factor was in each case a human voice. On Whit-Sunday, 21st May

[5] See *Journal of John Wesley*, I.475, note 2.
[6] Much as the theory attracts me, I remain sceptical, since the words which John Wesley uses to describe his conversion are so reminiscent of the eighth chapter of Romans as discussed in Luther's *Preface*.

THE UNALIENABLE FRIENDS

1738, as Charles Wesley lay a sick man, in the house of a Mr Bray, 'a poor ignorant mechanic who knows nothing but Christ, yet by knowing Him knows and discerns all things', Pentecost came to him. In the early morning his brother John and some friends had visited him, singing a hymn to the Holy Spirit which left him 'in hope and expectation of His coming'. Then as he was settling to sleep he heard a woman's voice distinctly say: 'In the name of Jesus of Nazareth arise and believe and thou shalt be healed of all thy infirmities.' At first he thought a Mrs Musgrave must have spoken the words, but when he discovered his mistake, he 'hoped it might be Christ indeed'. It was in fact Mrs Turner, the sister of Mr Bray, who had spoken under great constraint. Charles recorded all her inward promptings in his *Journal*, and he accepted her voice as the voice of God. 'I now found myself at peace with God and rejoiced in hope of loving Christ. . . . I saw that by faith I stood, by the continual support of faith which kept me from falling, though of myself I am ever sinking into sin.'

The instrument of John's conversion, as we have already seen, was also a human voice, but as with his brother, it spoke words which seemed divinely charged and applicable to his condition. The night of 24th May ended with the race of John Wesley through the darkened streets of London to tell his brother the good news. 'Towards ten', wrote Charles in his *Journal*, 'my brother was brought in triumph by a troop of our friends and declared "I believe".' They sang together 'with great joy' the great hymn Charles had composed two days before: 'Where shall my wondering soul begin? How shall I all to heaven aspire?' and they parted with prayer. Charles finished the *Journal* entry for that memorable day: 'At midnight I gave myself up to Christ, assured I was safe, sleeping or waking. Had continual experience of His power to overrule all temptation: and confessed with joy and surprise, that He was able to do exceeding abundantly for me, above what I can ask or think.' The Methodist Revival had begun.

In these early experiences, the bonds between the two brothers were drawn so tightly, that even in their alternation of moods, both in Georgia and London, there was the closest correspondence. In both of them the earlier sense of duty gave way to disillusionment and was closely followed by a sense of failure and despair, to be succeeded by a new hope excited by Peter Böhler and a hunger for that new relationship with God which only faith could give. For both of them conversion was the climax of long months of anxious seeking, and in both cases there was an instantaneous perception of God's unmerited grace and of the need for faith alone. In a moment of time they gave themselves wholly by faith to God, and never afterwards could they doubt the efficacy of that commitment.

THE UNALIENABLE FRIENDS

In later years the brothers diverged in their views on ecclesiastical polity, but never did they disagree on Christian doctrine with its proper evangelical emphasis. It was on Order, never on Faith, that the brothers knew any sort of tension, and that is why Charles stayed by his brother's side until the end. Even at a time when he was sorely troubled by the ecclesiastical irregularity of his brother, he could still write, in words which strangely move the heart,

> *My first and last unalienable friend,*
> *A brother's thoughts with due regard attend,*
> *A brother, still as thy own soul beloved.*

CHAPTER FOUR

Brothers in Battle

THE PARTNERSHIP that had its beginnings in Oxford, and developed in the testings of Georgia and in their hungry seeking after God, was finally confirmed in the prosecution of a holy war. Together John and Charles Wesley went out into the unknown that others might share their experience and engage with them in the service of God.

It was George Whitefield who applied the spark to the tinder. The break with the Moravians arose because the Fetter Lane Society became infected with 'stillness' and depreciated 'the means of grace'. John, who was later to tell his people categorically to wait upon the ordinances of God, took his little flock back to the Foundery, and so came that final rupture which set him free for a larger life. When Whitefield then wrote telling him of the fields white unto harvest in Bristol it was a summons coming at precisely the providential moment. There had been the break with the Moravians; the London Churches were closed to Charles and himself; it remained only to consult the Fetter Lane Society. By the casting of lots Charles's fears and his own misgivings were allayed. On 29th March 1739 he set off to Bristol and heard George Whitefield address great multitudes in the open air both at Bristol and Kingswood.

Was it really a surprise to him when he heard Whitefield at the close of the Sunday evening service (1st April 1739) in Bristol announce that John Wesley would preach the next day, after his own departure for America, in the brickyard at the end of St Philip's Plain? On Monday 2nd April at four o'clock in the afternoon, he took his stand in the open air and the great crusade had begun. In his own words, he 'consented to be more vile and proclaimed in the highways the glad tidings of salvation to about three thousand people'. The text he chose was a manifesto in itself: 'The Spirit of the Lord is upon me, because He had anointed me to preach the Gospel to the poor: He hath sent me to heal the broken-hearted, to preach deliverance to the captive, and recovery of sight to the blind, to set at liberty them that are bruised, to preach the acceptable year of the Lord.'

It was only a few weeks later that Charles was initiated into open-air preaching. On 29th May 1739 he was invited by Franklyn, a farmer, to preach in his field. He did so to about five hundred people and 'returned to the house rejoicing'. Even so, this was but the eaglet trying his wings; it was not until Saturday 24th June, St John Baptist's day, that he found he had full power to fly. After prayer he 'went forth in the name of Jesus Christ' and found near 'ten thousand helpless sinners waiting for the word in Moorfields'. He announced as his text: 'Come unto me all ye that travail and are heavy laden, and I will give you rest.' He found that the Lord was with him; his load was gone and all his doubts and scruples. The brothers had started on their journey and England was before them.

At this stage Charles Wesley was so much of one mind with his brother that, after a sermon on justification preached before the University of Oxford, he found himself criticized by the Dean and the Heads of colleges for his intemperate zeal and especially in 'preaching abroad, expounding in houses and singing psalms'. But though the last open-air preachers in this country, the Lollards, had suffered persecution and often martyrdom, Charles was as fully committed to field preaching as his brother John.

What were the principal reasons for the intense hostility which this open-air speaking aroused? In the first place it was a clear break with existing convention, and in particular meant the ignoring of parish boundaries and the wishes of the incumbents. This of itself was bound to rouse not only the anger of many parsons but also the displeasure of bishops. The offence was increased rather than reduced by the spectacle of two scholarly clergymen, correct in dress and cultivated in speech, pursuing irregular practices with an exquisite courtesy which disguised an inflexible determination of will.

Another reason for antagonism was that they

preached great experiential truths to an age which abhorred 'enthusiasm'. It was the great Bishop Butler himself who said that to claim inspiration of the Holy Spirit was 'a horrid thing, sir, a very horrid thing'. The brothers themselves were not violent in either manner or voice, though their preaching, especially that of Charles, was not cold or unimpassioned. A reading of their sermons is sufficient to disprove those who contended that they won their way by emotional appeal. No sermons rested more solidly upon biblical exegesis, and if by their natural but lively delivery they commended their message to the heart, the slow building up of the argument to its climax was a sustained address to the reason. The very novelty, however, of the occasion and of the evangelical truths proclaimed combined to produce revivalist phenomena which were as distasteful to the brothers Wesley as they were to their critics. Charles indeed recorded in his *Journal* (4th June 1743) that '*outward affections* were easy to be imitated', and claimed he had detected many counterfeits. 'Today, one who came from the alehouse, drunk, was pleased to fall into a fit for my entertainment, and beat himself heartily. I thought it a pity to hinder him; so, instead of singing over him, as had been often done, we left him to recover at his leisure. . . . Some very unstill sisters, who always took care to stand near me, and tried which should cry loudest, since I had them removed out of my sight, have now been as quiet as lambs.' John was not quite so sceptical as Charles and was inclined to consider that some of the phenomena were 'beyond the ordinary course of nature'.

When the novelty had died down, the uglier excesses of emotionalism also died away. Nevertheless an unpleasant impression lingered for many years. Robert Southey, in his classic life of John Wesley, did not hesitate to devote the whole of one chapter to Methodist extravagances, and certainly much of the clerical hostility was aggravated by repugnance to these early excesses.

The third and chief reason for opposition to the Wesleys was the unsettled nature of the times and the fear engendered by a quickly rising sect whose meetings were largely hidden from the public eye. What happened when these Methodists were in 'bands' and 'classes' or in their night 'society meetings'? What did the practice of weekly fasts on Fridays betoken? Were these lay preachers agents engaged on a sinister mission? If even Bishop Lavington of Exeter could write three volumes on *The Enthusiasm of Methodists and Papists Compared*, was it surprising that ordinary people should likewise feel that Methodism and Romanism had much in common? There were wild rumours that the brothers were Papists in disguise, and during the early years of the seventeen forties, when spy fever was at its height and any stranger not content to stay in his own locality was darkly regarded, it is not surprising that John Wesley was thought by some to be the head of a large and subversive movement. Charles Wesley was actually in danger of arrest at Wakefield (15th March 1744) because, so Justice Burton thought, 'we constantly pray for the Pretender in all our societies or nocturnal meetings'.[1] A warrant issued to the constable in Birstal asked him to summon 'Mary Castle of Birstal and all such other persons as you are informed can give any information against one Wesley or any other of the Methodist speakers, for speaking any treasonable words or exhortations as praying for the banished or the Pretender etc. to appear before me. . . .' Charles Wesley, together with the witnesses, appeared before the magistrates, and would not depart until they had acknowledged that his loyalty was unquestionable.

Undoubtedly these major reasons can be given for a decade of persecution, but a more immediate cause of violence was the fact that the mobs were so often plied with ale and goaded to fury by the squire and the parson. The rougher elements, thus egged on, took to this new sport very much as they might have indulged in bear-baiting. As the instigators often discovered, however, it is easier to excite a crowd than later to control it, and the

[1] The reference is to Bonnie Prince Charlie, the last of the exiled Stuarts, who landed in Scotland in 1745 in a desperate but unsuccessful bid to seize the British throne.

SONS TO SAMUEL

Wesleys often went in danger of their lives. The extreme fierceness of rioting was mainly confined to Staffordshire and Cornwall, though sporadic savage outbursts occurred elsewhere.

The persecution lasted ten years, but despite all that tormentors could do, this decade was one of astonishing growth, because of the leadership of the two brothers and the inspiring example they offered to their heroic and devoted followers. Three qualities shown by the brothers on many occasions saved them from serious injury if not from death, and nerved their people to like resistance. In the first place they knew intuitively that you must never turn your back on the enemy; always they looked the crowd in the face and if the mob had any obvious leader they gave him their particular attention. Secondly, they never succumbed to fear. Living before the days of psychiatry, they yet knew that fear begets attack and that timidity will at once throw your opponent into a mood of aggressiveness. Thirdly, they remained masters of the situation even when missiles were flying or the hubbub made speech impossible or they were being led to the magistrates.

Where illustrations abound only the most remarkable need be noted. To the north-east of Birmingham lay the small town of Wednesbury, and here there were scenes of wildest riot and fine heroism. John Wesley had formed a Society in 1753 which had quickly reached three hundred, but in the short interval between his departure and the coming of Charles Wesley, the antagonism of the mob had been quickened by the clergy. When Charles Wesley finished his meetings at Walsall he knew as he approached Wednesbury that he was coming into 'the mouth of hell'. However, as he came into the town accompanied by a number of Methodists all the company burst into song. Doubtless they sang one of his 'hymns of a time of tumult', and maybe as they walked through the surging crowds to the market-house steps, they sang

> *Though the sons of night blaspheme,*
> *More there are with us than them;*
> *God with us, we cannot fear;*
> *Fear, ye fiends, for Christ is here!*

As soon as he began to preach there was a shower of missiles. He was pushed from the steps and three times thrown down. Nothing daunted he got up once more, and after calmly pronouncing the Benediction he was allowed to pass through the crowd without further molestation.

Shortly after this incident, a party of Wednesbury Methodists were returning from Darlaston singing hymns as was their custom. They were pelted with stones and dirt, and the houses of Methodists in Wednesbury, Darlaston and West Bromwich suffered grievous damage. Although the mobs included contingents from Darlaston, Walsall and Bilston, and in their massed strength defied public order, the local Walsall magistrate, when requested for a warrant to apprehend the rioters, only threw his hat in the air and cried 'Hurrah'. The curate of Walsall actually encouraged the mob as though they were engaged in some holy crusade. As soon as John Wesley heard of the persecution in Staffordshire he came into the very midst of the rioting, but his good offices were of no avail and for some months preaching was confined to private houses.

This was an intolerable situation for Wesley, and once again, on 20th October 1743, he entered the lion's den at Wednesbury. It was an unforgettable day in Methodist annals. Whilst he was writing in the afternoon at the house of Francis Ward, a mob outside clamoured: 'Bring out the minister.' He asked what they wanted, and hearing it was to take him to the Justice, he said he would go with all his heart. But the Wednesbury magistrate was unwilling to see them, and in the gathering darkness and heavy rain they pressed on to Walsall. Once more the magistrate refused to see them, and they had to set back after a fruitless journey. They were pursued by a Walsall mob and Wesley was delivered into the hands of 'victorious ruffians'. He was beaten by an oak club, struck on the mouth and dragged by the hair. From one end of Walsall to the other he was paraded as a public spectacle. When his words availed nothing he began to pray, and the seeming miracle happened. The leader of the mob, who against his will must have been impressed by the unflinching courage of Wesley, suddenly turned and said: 'Sir, I will spend my life for you; follow me and no one shall hurt a hair of your head.' Together with a few companions he bore him safely through the astonished crowds and Wesley came safely to Wednesbury just before ten o'clock. Although for six hours he had been in peril of his life, his only comment was that he lost one flap of his waistcoat and a little skin from one hand. 'From beginning to end', he said, 'I found the same presence of mind as if I had been sitting in my own study.'

There is a fascinating sequel to the story. When Charles Wesley came to Wednesbury five days later, he found 'honest Munchin', the leader of the rabble, who had ultimately rescued John Wesley from his own fellow rioters, in a totally different role. He had been so moved by John Wesley's conduct on that day that he wanted to become a Methodist, and now, five days later, Charles Wesley received him as a member on trial. 'What thought you of my brother,' said Charles. 'Think of him?' said Munchin. 'I thought he was a man of God, and God was on his side, when so many of us could not kill one man.'

There were still further scenes of violence, especially in Darlaston; and at Wednesbury the rioting early in 1744 lasted for six days. Yet the persecuted

SONS TO SAMUEL

Methodists could write: 'We keep meeting together morning and evening, are in great peace and love with each other, and are nothing terrified by our adversaries. God grant we may endure to the end.'

That prayer was certainly answered. Persecution proved an excellent forcing-ground for Methodist societies. When Wesley paid his last visit but one to Wolverhampton, he recollected the wild scenes in his first visits and commented: 'What a den of lions this was for many years. But now it seems the last shall be first.'

Charles, writing in his *Journal* (25th October 1743) of his brother's fortitude amidst the violence of the mobs, declared: 'His feet never once slipped; for in their hands the angels bore him up. In the intervals of tumult, he spoke, the brethren assured me, with as much composure and correctness as he used to do in their Societies. The Spirit of glory rested on him.'

That summer (18th July 1743) Charles Wesley had already, in St Ives, Cornwall, 'come to the place of battle with the enemy set in array against us'. As he began the hundredth psalm they beat their drums and then ran on him, crying that he should not preach, and tried to pull him down. But Charles recorded in his *Journal* that they had no power to touch him. 'My soul was calm and fearless. I shook the dust off my feet and walked leisurely through the thickest of them, who followed like ramping and roaring lions, but their mouth was shut.'

Five days later, in that same town, Charles recorded that at an evening indoor gathering 'they came upon us like roaring lions headed by the Mayor's son'. This ringleader struck out all the candles and began 'courageously' beating the women. With great tact and presence of mind Charles Wesley laid his hand on him and appealed to him as a gentleman to restrain those who would hurt poor helpless women. This appeal to his honour so transformed the bully that 'he was turned into a friend immediately and laboured the whole time to quiet his associates'. Nothing daunted by these terrifying experiences, Charles Wesley gave out his text next morning: 'Thou shalt break forth on the right hand and on the left. . . . Fear not; for thou shalt not be ashamed: neither be thou confounded; for thou shalt not be put to shame: . . . Behold, I have created the smith . . . and the waster to destroy. No weapon that is formed against thee shall prosper' (Isaiah $54^{3-4, \ 16-17}$).

The utter fearlessness of John was never better shown than at Falmouth (4th July 1745) when he visited a sick woman and found almost at once that the house was surrounded by an innumerable multitude of people who cried: 'Bring out the Canorum.'[2] By and by the inner door gave way; at once John Wesley stepped forward and said: 'Here I am. Which of you has anything to say to me? To which of

---

[2] Derived from the Cornish 'canor', a singer—a reference to the love of singing among Methodists.

you have I done any wrong? To you? Or you?' He continued speaking till he came, bareheaded as he was (for he purposely left his hat, that they might all see his face), into the middle of the street, and then, raising his voice, said: 'Neighbours, countrymen, do you desire to hear me speak?' They cried vehemently: 'Yes, yes. He shall speak. Nobody shall hinder him.'

This whole incident offers the finest example of that composure in dealing with mobs which Charles and he continued to show until at length squire and parson grew ashamed of their spleen and crowds grew weary of their fun. The decade ended with the terrible riots in Cork (May 1750). By that time persecution had profited the brothers, because the Methodist people had received nation-wide publicity, and those who marvelled at their courage were more disposed to listen to their teaching. The sober sections of the community were appalled by the insensate action of magistrates who allowed the mobs to wreak their vengeance on the unoffending Methodist. There was therefore a certain revulsion of feeling, and it was aided by the failure of the Young Pretender and the settling down of the country to normal life. The brothers had triumphed. Revival was in the air.

After this decade of persecution the fourth and last phase of the partnership began with the marriage of Charles to Sarah Gwynne in 1749, and it ended only with his death. This is the period in which the younger brother ceased to itinerate and lived first in Bristol and later in London.

John never ceased to deplore this step and in sharper mood could almost regard it as a retrogression. This might lead the unwary to imagine that when Charles married and the children continued to come, his assistance to John was greatly lessened. Nothing could be farther from the truth; the manner of the help changed considerably, but the dimensions were as great as ever.

Indeed, for the first seven years after marriage he continued to make certain missionary tours both in the North and West, and even after he had ceased to itinerate he gave oversight to the Methodist societies in Bristol and, as he was able, in the West Country. Since Newcastle-upon-Tyne, London and Bristol were ever the three foci of Methodist enterprise, Charles was rendering invaluable service to the common cause by watching over Methodism in the West.

Nevertheless John desired to see more of his brother. In 1766 he said: 'I think you and I have abundantly too little intercourse with each other. Are we not old acquaintances? Have we not known each other for half a century? Are we not jointly engaged in such a work as probably no other two men on earth are? Why then do we keep such a distance? Is it a mere device of Satan? But surely

SONS TO SAMUEL

we ought not at this time to be ignorant of his devices. Let us therefore make the full use of the little time that remains. We, at least, should think aloud and use to the uttermost the light and grace on each bestowed. We should help each other.

> *Of little life the best to make*
> *And manage wisely the last stake.*'

In 1771 Charles moved with his family to London, and for the last seventeen years of his life was able to help his brother at the headquarters of their work. John had been deeply distressed by the passing of his sister Emily who, first at the Foundery and later at West Street Chapel, had given herself to the services of the Chapel and the welfare of the Society. Charles came therefore at an opportune moment, because he could supply a guiding hand over the Societies during those long months when John was absent from the capital.

Since 1739 the Foundery had been the centre of London Methodism, but in 1743 another chapel was found at West Street near the Seven Dials, and meeting-places were later opened at Snowfields, Southwark, and Spitalfields.[3] These were all served by Charles Wesley, but in 1778 the 'New Chapel', now known as Wesley's Chapel in the City Road,

---

[3] In *The History of City Road Chapel*, S. J. Stevenson records that when the new chapel was opened, the societies at West Street, Westminster, Spitalfields and Snowfields, Southwark, contributed to the general fund.

was opened. Henceforward Charles gave the greater part of his time to its ministrations. Only ordained clergymen were allowed to administer the Sacrament, and Charles Wesley with a little clerical assistance had to serve all the hundreds of London Methodists who came regularly to the Lord's Table. He took the daily morning and evening prayers as often as his health would allow, and he constantly took the two services on a Sunday.

This was an eloquent tribute to his vigour and enthusiasm, but somewhat of a reflection on his common sense. There were able preachers in London who fretted at the lack of opportunity to preach in the new 'cathedral' of Methodism, and their annoyance was heightened by the rigid stand taken by Charles on the question of Sacraments. Even a man like John Pawson, who had been ordained by John Wesley to administer the Sacrament in Scotland, was not allowed when he returned to London to officiate at the Lord's Table. In an outburst of anger he told a friend in 1787: 'We are just to be what we were before we came to Scotland—no Sacraments, no gowns, no nothing at all of any kind whatsoever.' Apart from Pawson, the men stationed in London were Thomas Rankin, Thomas Tennant and Peter Jaco; they were all connexionally known and respected, and all were outstanding preachers. So irate were they at Charles Wesley's consenting to share the pulpit only with episcopally ordained clergymen that they rebelled against this virtual monopoly. In the Conference of 1779 a decrease of 123 members was reported, and in the October of that year John Wesley, after his examination of the London Society, found it was due to 'a senseless jealousy that has crept in between our preachers'. A deputation of the trustees of the Chapel waited on Charles to request that the pulpit be occupied occasionally by other Methodist preachers. To this proposal he gave consent, and at once there was peace and growth in the Society.

Almost to the last months of his life Charles Wesley remained the faithful shepherd, counsellor and minister in charge of the London Societies. In his early day he was, in his impassioned eloquence, as effective a preacher as his brother. He was the master of the short staccato sentence which, infused by his natural vigour, could strike like a hammer blow on the conscience of his hearers. In 1766 John Wesley with his customary shrewdness noted their contrasted styles of preaching. 'O insist everywhere on *full* redemption', he said, 'receivable by *faith alone!* Consequently to be looked for *now*. You are *made*, as it were, for this very thing. Just here you are in your element. In connexion I beat you; but in strong, pointed *sentences* you beat me. Go on, in your *own way*, what God has peculiarly called you to. Press the *instantaneous* blessing: then I shall have more time for my peculiar calling, enforcing the *gradual* work.' Henry Morris's pithy summary declared that 'John's preaching was all principles, Charles's was all aphorisms'. This vehemence did not altogether desert him in old age, for Dr Coke and Henry Moore used freely to tell of a memorable occasion when, before Charles was half-way through his sermon, the free exercise of his arms, aided by the loose gown sleeves, caused the hymn-book to be swept off the pulpit so that it landed squarely on the head of Dr Coke who was sitting in the reading-desk beneath. The good doctor, looking up in pained surprise, was in time to catch the Bible which a little later was swept off the pulpit whilst the preacher still maintained the full flight of his inspiration. It was only after the service that he was told to his astonishment what had happened. No wonder that Henry Moore in his autobiography could speak of Charles Wesley's 'vehement and headstrong elocution'.

During all these years in Bristol and London Charles Wesley attended the annual Conferences, and in later years strove to restrain his brother from irregular ecclesiastical actions which would hasten that separation which even Charles realized to be inevitable. Since John was at this same period subject to the strong pressure of the younger preachers who had scant regard for the history, ritual and claims of the Established Church, his brother's restraining hand was providential. It delayed the separation long enough for Methodism to become a Church and not a sect, and it enabled Methodists in the next century to value their close links with the Church of England and the inheritance which had come through that association. The pressure of events and the continuing struggle for religious liberty drove Methodists in the later nineteenth century into alliance with the Free Churches, but they never forgot the rock from whence they were hewn. Charles, by his doggedness and conservatism, helped to mould the Methodist Church so that the mother can still be seen in the child.

Nor must it be forgotten that when he ceased itinerating he was able to increase the publication of his hymns. Regularly the books came out, and Henry Moore records that even at the close of his life he would come on his 'little horse grey with age' to the house in the City Road, and having left the horse in the garden would enter crying, 'Pen and ink, pen and ink'. When these were brought, he would sit down immediately and put to paper the hymn he had been composing on horseback. Only when this task was finished would he 'look round on those present and salute them with much kindness, ask after their health, give out a hymn and thus put all in mind of eternity'. Even on his deathbed he sought to express his thoughts in verse. He called his wife and dictated to her the last verse he ever composed:

BROTHERS IN BATTLE

In age and feebleness extreme,
Who shall a helpless worm redeem?
Jesus! my only hope Thou art,
Strength of my failing flesh and heart;
O could I catch one smile from Thee,
And drop into eternity!

When at last he came to die, his final thought was of his brother. He said, referring to a generous letter from John addressed to Charles junior, 'He will be kind to you when I am gone. I am certain your Uncle will be kind to all of you.' Most certainly that absolute confidence was justified. John Wesley and the Methodist people after him provided for all the needs of Mrs Charles Wesley and her daughter Sarah. When Adam Clarke invited Sarah Wesley in 1821 to assist him in the *Life of John Wesley* he was preparing, she wrote: 'His distinguished kindness to me from the earliest period I can remember made an indelible impression. I can retrace no word but of tenderness, no action but of condescension and generosity.' Then, as she warmed to her task, she said she could attest from experience that 'no human being was more alive to all the tender charities of domestic life than John Wesley'. In a revealing aside, she said that when the insanely jealous Mrs John Wesley was about to publish letters rifled from his bureau and grossly altered and misconstrued, her father set off to warn John Wesley, because 'the reputation of my Uncle was far dearer than his own'. Sally's letter to Adam Clarke spoke in every line of the love she felt for John because upon his brother's death he became a father to the three children. The Methodist Conference sustained the generosity of John, and the annuity settled on Mrs Charles Wesley was continued to her children after her death.

When John Wesley once remarked to his brother that no two men in Europe were doing a similar work, he was unduly modest both in reference to geography and time. In all the history of the Church there is not even a remote parallel to the story of what these two brothers accomplished for the Kingdom of God, sustaining each other by invincible affection, providing a foil for each other in temperament, and by their gifts each supplementing what the other could do. John was serene and even-tempered; Charles was fiery and liable to extremes of elation and depression. In this matter John was the constant goad, calling him out of his self-distrustfulness and opposing his own serene optimism to Charles's melancholy. In the 'business of saving souls' John was impatient of all obstacles and ready to try any fresh method of reaching the unchurched multitude. Charles was far more secure in his Anglican anchorage and acted as a useful brake upon his brother's impetuosity. In their different styles of preaching they each made their own distinct impact upon their hearers and together were the heralds of the Revival. In their ministry the itinerancy of John was essential to the growth of the Society, but first in Bristol and then in London, Charles shepherded the people and maintained an unrelaxing oversight of the work. Each of the brothers, however, had one supreme gift which he contributed separately, and these gifts added to the rest made possible the world-wide Methodist Church.

John had a genius for statesmanship which in Macaulay's famous words 'was scarce inferior to that of Richelieu'. He was the master Church builder. His connexional polity combined centralized authority with local freedom of movement; there was the giant's strength but it was not used tyrannously. It is rare for a centralized administration to retain flexibility. John Wesley moulded a Church, strong yet mobile and adaptable, to meet the changing circumstances of changing times.

Charles had an incomparable gift in religious verse. In that most laconic of all obituaries, containing a classic illustration of understatement, John said of his brother that 'his least praise was his talent for poetry', though he did of course add that the great Isaac Watts himself did not scruple to say that the single poem 'Wrestling Jacob' was worth all the verses he himself had written.

Those who delight in the ingenious but unprofitable exercise of deciding whether ultimately Charles's verses have not meant more to Christendom than all

John's manifold activities, might reflect that what God has joined together it is not wise to put asunder. As their lives were inextricably bound together, so of necessity was their work. Together they were the instruments of a Revival which has not yet ceased to re-fashion the lives of men. No other two men working throughout a long life-time together have brought such inestimable benefit to the Christian Church. Behind this common achievement was a love stronger than death, passing the love of woman. It was not by accident that when in 1760 John spoke of his brother and declared that 'all our lives and all God's dealings with us have been extraordinary from the beginning', he went on to quote David's words to Jonathan. In one short perfect sentence he wrote: 'I have a brother who is as my own soul.' It has been left for later generations to declare that they were lovely and pleasant in their lives and in death they were not divided.

CHAPTER FIVE

The Joint Manifesto

THE WORLD still awaits a book which will show the influence of politics on theology. In one sense even the greatest of reformers are the children of their age and are determined by its thought-forms; it is therefore not possible to deal adequately with the work of theologians except against the background of their times, and the contemporary modes of thinking.

The great leaders of the Reformation, Martin Luther and John Calvin, lived in an age which accepted Machiavelli's idea of the Prince. The Renaissance monarchs were brilliant in splendour and mighty in authority. This was popularly accepted as their right, and if any restraint was put upon them, it came from the nobles and not the people. This picture of the ideal prince affected the reformers' conception of God. It is true that Martin Luther, in his commentaries on Romans and Galatians for example, speaks of a love of God 'which does not find but creates the object of his love', and that Calvin, in his *Commentary on Romans*, can speak of that 'inappreciable love by which the Father refused not to bestow His Son for our salvation', and of the 'fountain of love which is in the Father and flows to us from Christ'; nevertheless, in both reformers the central emphasis is upon the sovereign majesty of God: *soli Deo gloria*. His glory is shown in His grace which flows undeserved and unmerited and can be received by faith alone. Philip Watson in his treatment of Luther's theology expounds 'the majesty of uncreated love', and argues that in it is found 'the essential righteousness and the unassailable sovereignty of God'. The same can be said, though in narrower terms, of Calvin's teaching on election and reprobation. In his *agape* God goes out in strong and sovereign activity. The final impression is of a King, plenteous in mercy and terrible in justice, who sits upon the throne of the universe.

It is not unkind to Luther to quote his pamphlet *Against the Murdering Thieving Hordes of Peasants*, in which he urges the princes to stab and strangle and slay, and adds that in such times 'a prince can merit heaven better by bloodshed than by prayer'. It is true that these words have been used by merciless detractors a thousand times to castigate the great reformer, and the present writer has no wish to be numbered in such company, but it is obvious that here was a final parting with the people whose cause represented for him anarchy, thievery and the sin of rebellion. Democracy had not yet appeared as a possible alternative to despotic or oligarchic rule, and so, despite Luther's acknowledgement of that divine love which, like the sun, shines on bad and good alike, he was not able to work out the democratic consequences. Quite certainly this was equally true of Calvin, who, speaking of the mercy by which some are elected to salvation, could speak also of that justice by which most are reprobated to eternal damnation.

The new distinctive contribution of John and Charles Wesley lay in their understanding of love in relation to God's nature and purpose.[1] They did not sacrifice or minimize any of the essential insights of Luther and Calvin. Both as interpreters of the Bible and as children of their age, they were able to conceive of God as lifted far above all rule and authority and power and dominion. He rules from His throne as King of Kings, and upon His strong selective activity we utterly depend. John and Charles Wesley gladly accepted the reformers' solemn bowing of the knee to God.

In the *Conference Minutes* of 1745 certain questions about Calvinism were proposed and answered.

Q. 22. Does not the truth of the gospel lie very near to both Calvinism and Antinomianism?

A. Indeed it does; as it were within a hair's breadth; so that it is altogether foolish and sinful because we do not quite agree with either one or the other to run from them as far as ever we can.

[1] In my book, *The Astonishing Youth*, I adumbrated the unique significance of God's love in the teaching of the Wesleys, and this chapter is an amplification of what I indicated there.

Q. 23. Wherein may we come to the very edge of Calvinism?

A. (1) In ascribing all good to the free grace of God.

(2) In denying all natural free will and all power antecedent to grace, and

(3) In excluding all merit from man, even for what he has or does by the grace of God. At the previous Conference there had been the frank confession that 'we have leaned too much towards Calvinism', but now came the resolute acceptance of the great truths of Calvinism except 'the horrible decrees'.

In his sermon on 'The Discoveries of Faith' John Wesley used language which might well have been that of Luther or Calvin: 'But I know by faith that above all these is the Lord Jehovah; He that is, that was, and that is to come, that is God from everlasting and world without end: He that filleth heaven and earth: He that is infinite in power, in wisdom, in justice, in mercy and in holiness: He that created all things, visible and invisible, by the breath of His mouth and still upholds them all, preserves them in being by the word of His power, and that governs all things that are in heaven above, in earth beneath and underneath the earth.' This too is the very language of Charles when he contemplates the transcendent majesty of God:

THE JOINT MANIFESTO

Thee the first-born sons of light,
  In choral symphonies,
Praise by day, day without night,
  And never, never cease;
Angels and archangels all
  Praise the mystic Three in One,
Sing, and stop, and gaze, and fall
  O'erwhelmed before Thy throne.

There was no denial of the Reformation truth that God is King, and that all comes by His grace. The supreme merit of the brothers was to enlarge the conception of God so that the King is also the Father, and the power He exercises is that of love. When John invaded the central citadel of Calvinists and preached on the text beloved by them (Romans 8^{29-30}), 'Whom he did foreknow, he also did predestinate to be conformed to the image of his Son, ... whom he did predestinate them he also called: and whom he called, them he also justified: and whom he justified, them he also glorified', he concluded his sermon with five simple propositions: (1) God knows all believers, (2) wills that they should be saved from sin, (3) to that end justifies them, (4) sanctifies, and (5) takes them to glory. This emphasis comes countless times in his brother's hymns:

To us He hath, in gracious love,
  An understanding given,

SONS TO SAMUEL

To recognize Him from above
The Lord of earth and heaven.

The self-existing God supreme,
Our Saviour we adore,
Fountain of life eternal, Him
We worship evermore.

The brothers received this new conception of God's sovereign love from three main sources. Firstly, they had been reared in Caroline High Churchmanship; they were familiar with the great mystical writers and they were versed therefore in the Catholic tradition and practice. Mr John M. Todd, in his book, *John Wesley and the Catholic Church*, has given us an able study of John Wesley's conscious and unconscious acceptance of Roman Catholic precept; but in the wider use of the term, John and Charles were heirs of a catholic legacy in discipline, doctrine and liturgy, and this saved them from the excesses of Calvinism. The heady wine of Reformation truth received via the Pietists and Moravians, was not the only draught to quench their thirst. Both in the Book of Homilies and in the Thirty-nine Articles they knew an Arminian Anglicanism which avoided the corruptions of Renaissance catholicism and softened the asperities of the Reformers.

Secondly, they lived in the century of Whig oligarchy which ended with the French Revolution across the Channel, and the use of stoutly democratic words

THE JOINT MANIFESTO

in England. The moderate constitutionalism of Locke had broadened through the writings of Godwin, Joseph Priestley and Tom Paine. The literary revival which dates from the Lyrical Ballads of Wordsworth and Coleridge sprang from the discovery of the importance of the ordinary man. John and Charles were children of their age, and could not easily think of God as the absolute despot when despotism was unfashionable. Their minds were opened, however, to a new understanding of God's truth; they were able to make a vital leap forward in theological thinking from an august sovereignty of divine grace to an 'amazing' and 'stupendous' love which holds within itself a manger, a cross, and an empty tomb.

Lastly, they were impelled to this fresh orientation of thought by the necessities of the missionary work which followed upon their evangelical conversion. The note was sounded in the hymn Charles Wesley wrote on the day after his conversion. He apprehends the nature of the God who has saved him:

> *O how shall I the goodness tell,*
> *Father, which Thou to me hast showed?*
> *That I, a child of wrath and hell,*
> *I should be called a child of God . . .*

and then he recognizes the imperative need for others to share such love:

SONS TO SAMUEL

Outcasts of men, to you I call,
Harlots, and publicans, and thieves!
He spreads His arms to embrace you all;
Sinners alone His grace receives.

It is not without cause that the first sermon in the Standard Edition is John Wesley's great trumpet call: 'By grace are ye saved through faith.' The grace comes from divinely 'free and undeserved favour', and by faith a man knows that nothing separates him from the love of God.

But these three predisposing factors would not have counted apart from the strongly original cast of thought in the brothers as they pondered over their Bibles in the light of their own experience. Incidentally, nothing illustrates so vividly their close intellectual sympathy as the identity of their ideas in the realm of theology. It is impossible to describe John's views without reference to the hymns of Charles, and it is equally necessary to illustrate the great themes of Charles's verse from the writings of his brother John.

The four distinctive ways in which the brothers thought of God's love were in relation to salvation, assurance, holiness, and fellowship. They dissented no whit from the classic expression of salvation as by grace alone on God's side and by faith alone on man's. For them, however, grace is but love in action, and we are saved only because the divine

THE JOINT MANIFESTO

Lover is bent upon our recovery. When John Wesley wrote the obituary notice of Charles for the *Minutes* of the 1788 Conference, in the three sentences he allowed himself he quoted Isaac Watts's remarkable tribute that Wrestling Jacob was worth all the verses he himself had written. In this treatment of the lonely Jacob wrestling all night at the brook Jabbok with his ghostly adversary, Charles Wesley affirms that the long night's agony brought victory because Jacob was able to know the heavenly wrestler's name, and because that name was love:

> *'Tis Love! 'tis Love! Thou diedst for me!*
>   *I hear Thy whisper in my heart;*
> *The morning breaks, the shadows flee,*
>   *Pure, universal Love Thou art;*
> *To me, to all, Thy mercies move:*
> *Thy nature and Thy name is Love.*

When Charles tries to express this love in words, his range of adjectives fail him. It is 'amazing', 'stupendous', 'unexampled', 'everlasting', 'immense', 'unsearchable'; but when all has been said, nothing is said, for the adjective which is meant to describe can only limit. He must leave the life to speak the message:

> *His thoughts and words and actions prove,*
> *His life and death—that God is love.*

So in one of his very greatest hymns he comes back to the fact that God loves because it is the nature of His Being. Such a love passes beyond the power of words to describe or minds to comprehend.

> *Love moved Him to die,*
> *And on this we rely;*
> *He hath loved, He hath loved us: we cannot tell why;*
> *But this we can tell,*
> *He hath loved us so well*
> *As to lay down His life to redeem us from hell.*

But why should He love at such incredible cost? Charles Wesley has only one final answer—'He hath loved, He hath loved us, because He would love'.

Salvation, then, can be understood in the categories of grace and faith so long as it is understood that grace is the downward reach of divine *agape* and faith is the upward reach of the human heart. Salvation is love answering to love, so that as God gives Himself to the seeker, the seeker gives himself to God, and in Philip Doddridge's strangely realistic phrase, 'the great transaction's done'. In his sermon 'The Almost Christian', John Wesley has no doubt that the first token of being altogether a Christian is the response to God's love which enables us to love Him with heart and soul and mind and strength. What does Justification by Faith mean, asks Wesley in his sermon on that subject, and he answers: that 'God will not inflict on a sinner what he deserved to suffer, because the Son of His love hath suffered for him. And from that time we are accepted through the Beloved. . . .' This is the very accent of Charles Wesley:

> *O let Thy love my heart constrain!*
>   *Thy love for every sinner free,*
> *That every fallen soul of man*
>   *May taste the grace that found out me;*
> *That all mankind with me may prove*
> *Thy sovereign everlasting love.*

In one great hymn he asks the question:

> *When shall Thy love constrain,*
> *And force me to Thy breast?*

then he states the grounds for asking that question, and finally gives his answer:

> *Nay, but I yield, I yield!*
> *I can hold out no more,*
> *I sink, by dying love compelled,*
> *And own Thee conqueror.*

The second fresh interpretation the brothers gave of the Father's love was in relation to 'the Witness of the Spirit', known by Methodists as the doctrine of Assurance. The ill-informed have commonly dismissed this particular emphasis as subjectivism. Dr Pusey, the eminent Tractarian, said sneeringly, 'Methodists believe in salvation by feeling'. But the grounds of this new standing with God were not sought in the emotions but in the objective facts of Christ's saving work. Because of His life and death and rising again and His ascent in glory, followed by the gift of the Holy Spirit, John and Charles Wesley could dare to believe that a man might have a conscious awareness of his new relationship to God. This seemed to them the plain evidence of Holy Scripture. When John was asked for the scriptural warrant for his 'strange' teaching, he declared: 'The Spirit Himself beareth witness with our spirit that we are the children of God', and again, in another sermon ('The Spirit of Bondage and of Adoption'), he quoted Paul's letter to the Romans once more: 'Ye have not received the spirit of bondage again to fear, but ye have received the Spirit of adoption, whereby we cry, "Abba, Father".'

This teaching was not clear in Romanism partly because of an over-stressed Sacramentalism and partly because no proper place was allowed for private judgement and therefore private awareness. The mystics, it is true, allowed a central place to the ecstasy of private communion with God, but they were sometimes tempted to exaggerate the emotional element and to be attached only loosely to the doctrinal standards of the faith. The Antinomians on the other hand were so amply satisfied with their new status as believers that they made 'the Law void' and neglected the appointed means of grace.

THE JOINT MANIFESTO

The Anglican Church accepted the doctrine, but refused to explore it and therefore failed to know its worth. In the Thirty-nine Articles (Art. XVII) it was taught that 'those who through grace obey the calling of God are made the sons of God by adoption', and Bishop Pearson in his notable *Exposition of the Creed* understood this to mean that the office of the Holy Ghost is to assure us of our adoption as sons. Nevertheless the Church of England never taught the witness of the Spirit as a privilege to be enjoyed by the believer. On the contrary, when the brothers began their work, nothing was more offensive to their fellow clergymen than this teaching on Assurance which laid them open to the odious charge of 'enthusiasm'.

In the statement of Presbyterian belief known as the 'Westminster Confession' (1648) there was a reference to assurance as the ordinary gift of the Spirit to the believer, but in Calvinist fashion, it was further held that once attained it was indefectible. This was another aspect of the final perseverance of the saints. What gave Calvinists their magnificent fighting qualities, on the battlefield and in the market-place alike, was not so much the assurance of salvation as the conviction that they were God's elect and no final harm could befall them.

The doctrine therefore was not new to the eighteenth century, but never before had it been firmly grounded in the saving mission of Christ as expounded in Holy Writ, and taught as a privilege to be accepted and enjoyed by the believer. The Scylla of mysticism and the Charybdis of antinomianism were alike avoided in the rational and scriptural exposition of the Wesleys; they believed they were only calling Christians back to neglected treasures in their faith.

They themselves first received it from the Moravians. John Wesley had been astonished at the calm of the twenty-six Moravians in the height of a violent storm on the *Simmonds*. From Peter Böhler he learnt that one result of faith in Christ was 'constant peace arising from a sense of forgiveness'. In his *Journal* he confessed his amazement and declared that he looked upon it as a new gospel. When on 24th May 1738 he was converted and set down his experience of salvation, he used the very language of Assurance—'an assurance was given me that He had taken away *my* sins, even *mine*, and saved *me* from the law of sin and death'. It is curious how other members of his family had enjoyed this experience without making it explicit in doctrinal terms. According to Susanna, her father Dr Annesley had known the experience, without however preaching it to others. She herself told her son on 3rd September 1739 that as she was receiving the Holy Sacrament she knew the witness of the Spirit. The old Rector on his death-bed had said in unforgettable words to John: 'The inward witness, son, the inward witness, that is proof, the strongest proof of Christianity.'

THE JOINT MANIFESTO

Although in late years John did not insist that this ought to be the invariable consequence of salvation, he did affirm to the very end that it ought to be a 'common privilege of real Christians'.

But what was the standing of which the Christian was assured by the witness of the Spirit? At a minimum he knew that his sins had been forgiven, but when fully assured he knew that he was now in the household of faith. To describe this experience John Wesley repeatedly makes use of the Pauline word 'adoption', and claims that the believer can rejoice because he is no longer in bondage but in freedom; he is no longer a slave but a son. But what precisely does this involve? John Wesley says it means that the believer 'loves, delights, and rejoices in God'. In response to God's love the sinner is saved and by the witness of the Spirit he is assured of that love. The conclusion of his noble translation from Gerhard Tersteegen's '*Verborgne Gottesliebe du*' shows that even in 1736 John was yearning for an explicit assurance of God's love:

> *Speak to my inmost soul, and say,*
> *I am thy Love, thy God, thy All!*
> *To feel Thy power, to hear Thy voice,*
> *To taste Thy love, be all my choice.*

In his translation of Antoinette Bourignon's hymn he anticipates again the later formulation of his views on Assurance:

SONS TO SAMUEL

> *Thee I can love, and Thee alone,*
> *With pure delight and inward bliss:*
> *To know Thou tak'st me for Thine own,*
> *O what a happiness is this!*

In the flood tide of the Revival John Wesley left his brother Charles to catch the ecstasy of this new state in lyrical verse:

> *Inspire the living faith*
> *Which whosoe'er receives,*
> *The witness in himself he hath,*
> *And* consciously *believes.*

And what can the believer consciously experience? The full answer comes in another hymn on the Holy Spirit:

> *Where the indubitable seal*
>   *That ascertains the Kingdom mine?*
> *The powerful stamp I long to feel,*
>   *The signature of love divine;*
> *O shed it in my heart abroad,*
> *Fullness of love, of heaven, of God.*

Most descriptive of all is a hymn wholly given to an assurance that Jesus is ours and that we can rejoice in his love:

> *My God, I am Thine;*
> *What a comfort divine,*
> *What a blessing to know that my Jesus is mine!*

THE JOINT MANIFESTO

In the heavenly Lamb
Thrice happy I am,
And my heart it doth dance at the sound of His name.

True pleasures abound
In the rapturous sound;
And whoever hath found it hath paradise found.
My Jesus to know,
And feel His blood flow,
'Tis life everlasting, 'tis heaven below.

Yet onward I haste
To the heavenly feast:
That that is the fullness; but this is the taste;
And this I shall prove,
Till with joy I remove
To the heaven of heavens in Jesus's love.

In another memorable hymn he sounds this same note of assurance of God's love and of His presence:

My God! I know, I feel Thee mine,
And will not quit my claim,
Till all I have is lost in Thine
And all renewed I am.

But those who would know the full teaching of Charles on Assurance must read the whole of two of his greatest hymns devoted throughout to its exposition. In the one, 'Thou great mysterious God unknown', he asks that he may not stop at knowing only God's fear, but go on to know His 'sweet forgiving love'. He declares that if he had this inward witness he would have the antepast of heaven;

> *And should I not with faith draw nigh,*
> *And boldly Abba, Father! cry*
> *And know myself Thy child?*

In the second hymn he deliberately starts with the all-important question,

> *How can a sinner know*
> *His sins on earth forgiven?*

And then in succeeding verses he shows not only how the experience may come but in what it consists. It is the assurance of God's love which is stronger than death:

> *Exults our rising soul,*
> *Disburdened of her load*
> *And swells unutterably full*
> *Of glory and of God.*
>
> *His love, surpassing far*
> *The love of all beneath,*
> *We find within our hearts, and dare*
> *The pointless darts of death.*

The brothers taught together a doctrine of assurance which offered the believer the priceless privilege of knowing God's love and rejoicing in it. It was

THE JOINT MANIFESTO

because the Methodists accepted the teaching gladly that England became 'a nest of singing birds'.

The third great emphasis on God's love has become the very corner-stone of Methodist theology, and in a recent book on the subject Dr Eric Baker has spoken of 'the unique place of the doctrine of Christian Perfection in the Methodist tradition'. John Wesley within a few short months of his death looked back reflectively and said: 'This doctrine is the grand depositum which God has lodged with the people called Methodists; and for the sake of propagating this chiefly He appears to have raised us up.' On more than one occasion throughout his life he declared that where scriptural holiness was not preached the Societies would languish.

As early as the Conference of 1744 John Wesley declared that holiness is to love God with all our heart and soul and mind and strength, and our neighbour as ourselves. Yet the same Wesley could say that the 'pure love of God shed abroad in the heart destroys every bitter root and temper of sin'. These two statements apparently conflict with each other, for in the one case the emphasis is upon the love of man for God and in the second the love of God for man. Nevertheless the difference is more apparent than real, because both statements are true. There is both the downward reach of God's love and the entire response in love of the believer. In his *Plain Account of Christian Perfection* (1777) John

Wesley quoted in full his brother's hymn, 'Lord, I believe a rest remains'. One verse which does not appear in the present *Methodist Hymn-book* speaks of the wholehearted plea of the believer for God to possess his soul. Here is an illustration of the love of God which can only possess the heart when in his entire love for God the individual allows Him to enter fully:

> *Come, O my Saviour, come away!*
> *Into my soul descend!*
> *No longer from Thy creature stay,*
> *My Author and my End.*

This is why John Wesley was never happy in the use of such phrases as Sinless or Entire Perfection, and why he chose rather to speak of Scriptural Holiness or Perfect Love.

When he thought of sin as 'a voluntary transgression of a known law', he asserted that a man, by God's grace, could be more than conqueror. In this one respect he could share his brother's optimism, though he could never believe with Charles that the 'seed of sin's disease' might be removed. John realized that apart from voluntary transgressions there was an inherent 'sinfulness' in human nature from which no man could wholly be freed. So he modified his earlier extravagant claims about sinless perfection and expressed the conviction that only at the moment of death did the vast majority of

THE JOINT MANIFESTO

Christians know a totally incorrupt devotion to God.

Was the experience of perfect love instantaneous or gradual? John had no doubt that for some the change was instantaneous, yet that even so, a 'man still grows in grace, in the knowledge of Christ, in the love and image of God, and will do so, not only till death, but to all eternity'. This led him to say that holiness 'is improvable', for one 'perfected in love may grow in grace far swifter than he did before'. The conclusion of this classic statement of the Methodist doctrine of holiness is that 'we expect to love God with all our heart and our neighbour as ourselves, because He will in this world cleanse the thoughts of our hearts by the inspiration of His Holy Spirit that we shall perfectly love Him and worthily magnify His holy Name'.

This really is the conception of holiness as fellowship with God in which there is reciprocity of fullest love. That is why John Wesley brushed aside almost impatiently the question, 'Is it sinless?' 'It is not worth while', he said, 'to contend for a term. It is salvation from sin.' Actually the question did not accord with his categories of thought. There is a perfection of the acorn but it is not the perfection of the oak. Change there must be, for a personal relationship with God must deepen with the years if the fellowship is to be real. Even so there will be the dark nights of the soul when all that matters is not our grasp of God but His strong hold of us.

Sin, however, would be the deliberate breaking of that union, and holiness would be the whole response of the believer to the love of God in the intimacy of deepening fellowship.

It is because John Wesley conceived of holiness in this positive, vital, organic way, that Methodism differs so entirely from those splinter sects in Protestantism which make a cult of holiness. They differ from each other only in the varying degrees of severity in which they construe their separation from the world. Holiness for them is a series of do's and don'ts, imperatives and prohibitions. The consequence is that holiness is drawn up in legal terms even if the Law be that of Moses. Commonly there is a smell of the charnel house about it, because there is such steady emphasis on the mortification of the flesh. It is refreshing to turn from such perfectionism to the teaching of John Wesley on the love of God which can possess a man wholly, so that in the answering completeness of his own love for God he comes to that holiness which is wholeness of living.

This note was caught magically in Charles Wesley's hymns. In the famous 1780 *Collection of Hymns for the Use of the People called Methodists*, it is the long section on believers groaning for full redemption which displays most revealingly the close accord of Charles with John in the treatment of holiness. Always, for him, holiness means the intimate fellowship with God whereby His almighty love calls forth the fullest response from the believing heart; the perfect love of God awakens the perfect love of man.

> *Let us, to perfect love restored*
> *Thy image here retrieve,*
> *And in the presence of our Lord,*
> *The life of angels live.*

In the hymn 'Come, Holy Ghost, all quickening fire!' there is a verse no longer sung which interprets triumphantly the Wesley's teaching on assurance and on perfect love:

> *Thy witness with my spirit bear,*
> *That God, my God, inhabits there;*
> *Thou, with the Father, and the Son,*
> *Eternal light's co-eval beam;*
> *Be Christ in me, and I in Him,*
> *Till perfect we are made in one.*

In a shorter metre and with a fine blend of Latin and Anglo-Saxon words he swings to the same conclusion:

> *Jesus, Thine all-victorious love*
> *Shed in my heart abroad;*
> *Then shall my feet no longer rove,*
> *Rooted and fixed in God. . . .*

> *Love can bow down the stubborn neck*
> *The stone to flesh convert;*
> *Soften, and melt, and pierce, and break,*
> *An adamantine heart. . . .*

SONS TO SAMUEL

My steadfast soul, from falling free,
Shall then no longer move;
But Christ be all the world to me,
And all my heart be love.

If one must make an end where there is no end, let a one-verse hymn express Charles Wesley's view of holiness as love answering fully to love:

Give me the enlarged desire,
And open, Lord, my soul,
Thy own fullness to require,
And comprehend the whole:
Stretch my faith's capacity
Wider and yet wider still;
Then with all that is in Thee
My soul for ever fill!

There is a disposition on the part of Methodist theologians to speak only of the Wesley brothers' emphasis on salvation, assurance and holiness; actually there is just as original an emphasis on fellowship, and this also is related by them to God's love. The love which, with undistinguishing regard, comprehends the whole race makes all mankind His by creation; the love which gave itself in a manger and on a Cross makes all believers His by redemption. And just as John Wesley rejected the kind of atomistic democracy envisaged both in France and England by extreme left-wing republicans, but believed

THE JOINT MANIFESTO

rather in an organic society informed by a common purpose, so he saw God's will to be not an aggregation of believers but a society of the redeemed. In his Sermon 'Of the Church', he asked himself a simple question—'What is the Church?'—and he returned a simple answer. It is 'all the persons in the universe whom God hath so called out of the world —as to be one body, united by one Spirit, having one faith, one hope, one baptism; and one God and Father of all, who is above all, and through all, and in them all'. God therefore, who calls men by His love, unites those who share that love into 'one body'.

In his great sermon on 'The Catholic Spirit', he steadily advances in argument to a conclusion which must be set down in full, since, in my submission, no ending of the published sermons of the truly great has ever surpassed its Christian charity and natural eloquence:

'If, then, we take this word in the strictest sense, a man of a catholic spirit is one who, in the manner above-mentioned, gives his hand to all whose hearts are right with his heart: one who knows how to value, and praise God for, all the advantages he enjoys, with regard to the knowledge of the things of God, the true scriptural manner of worshipping him, and, above all, his union with a congregation fearing God and working righteousness: one who, retaining these blessings with the strictest care, keeping them as the apple of his eye, at the same time loves—as friends, as brethren in the Lord, as members of Christ and children of God, and fellow heirs of his eternal kingdom—all, of whatever opinion or worship, or congregation, who believe in the Lord Jesus Christ; who love God and man; who, rejoicing to please, and fearing to offend God, are careful to abstain from evil, and zealous of good works. He is the man of a truly catholic spirit, who bears all these continually upon his heart; who, having an unspeakable tenderness for their persons, and longing for their welfare, does not cease to commend them to God in prayer, as well as to plead their cause before men; who speaks comfortably to them, and labours, by all his words, to strengthen their hands in God. He assists them to the uttermost of his power in all things, spiritual and temporal. He is ready "to spend and be spent for them"; yea, to lay down his life for their sake.

'Thou, O man of God, think on these things! If thou art already in this way, go on. If thou hast heretofore mistook the path, bless God who hath brought thee back! And now run the race which is set before thee, in the royal way of universal love. Take heed, lest thou be either wavering in thy judgement, or straitened in thy bowels: but keep an even pace, rooted in the faith once delivered to the saints, and grounded in love, in true catholic love, till thou art swallowed up in love for ever and ever!'

Christian fellowship is grounded therefore in our

THE JOINT MANIFESTO

common sharing of God's love which excites our mutual love. John Wesley believed so much in this love of the Head for the family and the family for one another that he made it the basis of his Church polity. Connexionalism is only fellowship spelt out in ecclesiastical terms. His people belonged to each other in their circuits, districts, and annual Conferences.

But this was no exclusive fellowship, for John Wesley taught them to be the friends of all, the enemies of none. When he preached on 'A caution against bigotry', he took as his text words from St Mark's Gospel (9^{38-9}) which carry their own message:

'And John answered him, saying, Master, we saw one casting out devils in thy name, and he followeth not us: and we forbad him, because he followeth not us. But Jesus said, Forbid him not.' In a notable passage in his sermon on the Catholic Spirit he discussed the beliefs which can divide Christians, but declared that they paled into insignificance in the light of God's love for them all and their family relationship to one another:

'I do not mean, "Embrace my modes of worship"; or, "I will embrace yours". This also is a thing which does not depend either on your choice or mine. We must both act as each is fully persuaded in his own mind. Hold you fast that which you believe is most acceptable to God, and I will do the same. I believe the Episcopal form of church government to be scriptural and apostolical. If you think the Presbyterian or Independent is better, think so still, and act accordingly. I believe infants ought to be baptized; and this may be done either by dipping or sprinkling. If you are otherwise persuaded, be so still, and follow your own persuasion. It appears to me, that forms of prayer are of excellent use, particularly in the great congregation. If you judge extemporary prayer to be of more use, act suitably to your own judgement. My sentiment is, that I ought not to forbid water, wherein persons may be baptized; and that I ought to eat bread and drink wine, as a memorial of my dying Master: however, if you are not convinced of this, act according to the light you have. I have no desire to dispute with you one moment upon any of the preceding heads. Let all these smaller points stand aside. Let them never come into sight. "If thine heart is as my heart," if thou lovest God and all mankind, I ask no more: "Give me thine hand." '

Charles accepted wholly this view of fellowship in the love of God. In a hymn for the society meeting, he declares:

> *Who of twain hast made us one,*
> *Maintains our unity:*
> *Jesus is the corner stone*
> *In whom we all agree.*
> *Servants of one common Lord,*
> *Sweetly of one heart and mind,*

THE JOINT MANIFESTO
Who can break a threefold cord
Or part whom God hath joined?

In a section of the 1780 book on the 'Communion of Saints' he interprets in verse the profoundest depth in Johannine thought:

> *Christ, our Head, gone up on high,*
> *Be Thou in thy Spirit nigh!*
> *Advocate with God, give ear*
> *To thine own effectual prayer!*
>
> *One the Father is with thee;*
> *Knit us in like unity;*
> *Make us, O uniting Son,*
> *One as Thou and He are one!* . . .
>
> *Fill us with the Father's love;*
> *Never from our souls remove;*
> *Dwell in us and we shall be*
> *Thine through all eternity.*

One must wrestle against the desire to keep on quoting those hymns on fellowship in which Charles Wesley is unsurpassed, and limit further mention of them to a few single lines which stand out as lightning indications of what fellowship must mean:

> '*Nourish us with social grace.*'
> '*Transcripts of thy holiness.*'
> '*Live and die wrapt up in thee!*'
> '*Saved by faith which works by love.*'

There, in a few words, is distilled the essence of his teaching.

There is a tendency in these days to find the distinctive Methodist contribution to theology in the Wesleys' teaching on the Holy Spirit. Certainly the person and office of the Holy Spirit appear prominently both in the writings and sermons of John and in the verse of Charles. How could it be otherwise? The miracle of the new birth is never accomplished by a man's 'decision' or 'surrender' or 'commitment'. First of all the work belongs to God. In the beginning there is the prevenient work of the Holy Spirit, and then the actual operation of grace—still through the Spirit—by which the rebirth takes place. Similarly it is through the Holy Spirit witnessing with our spirit that we know we are children of God; it is He alone who makes us know that we have been 'adopted' into God's family so that all its wealth is our own possession. Again, the love of God 'shed abroad in our hearts' may rightly be described in other words as the indwelling of the Holy Spirit, and in many hymns by Charles on holiness the reference is to the work of the Holy Spirit in the believer's heart:

> *Our heavenly Guide*
> *With us shall abide,*
> *His comforts impart,*
> *And set up His Kingdom of love in the heart.*

or more powerfully still:

> *Come, Holy Ghost, all-quickening fire,*
> *Come, and in me delight to rest;*
> *Drawn by the lure of strong desire,*
> *O come and consecrate my breast;*
> *The temple of my soul prepare,*
> *And fix Thy sacred presence there.*

Finally, it is the Holy Spirit whose function it is to bind men to God and to one another, so that as one speaks of the grace of the Lord Jesus Christ and the love of God, one speaks of the fellowship of the Holy Spirit. The apostolic benediction throws an ever-steady light on the work of the Holy Spirit within the Church. In a true sense, therefore, the Wesleys, in speaking of God's love in salvation, assurance, holiness, and fellowship, were remarking afresh upon the operation of the Holy Spirit.

But this is not a secondary emphasis, just as it is not a clouding of their fresh interpretation of God's love in the heart of the believer and the life of the Church. For both John and Charles Wesley the Christian faith was rooted in the triune God. Within the space of one sermon, or the limits of one hymn, John and Charles Wesley used 'God' and 'the Holy Spirit' as interchangeable terms. In one of his memorable hymns Charles Wesley speaks in successive verses of 'Abba Father', 'Heavenly Adam', 'Holy Ghost', and then concludes:

SONS TO SAMUEL

Spring of life, Thyself impart,
Rise eternal in my heart.

In the Holy Spirit, therefore, God comes in love that a man may be saved, comes in witness that a man may know he is saved, comes in fullness that a man may be wholly saved, comes in fellowship that a man may share his experience with others.

This was not new teaching, for if it was it could not have been Christian. It derived its strength from Reformation, Anglican, and Roman Catholic sources, and it had its ultimate roots in the New Testament. Nevertheless, though the content was not new, the assembling and balance and emphasis were new. Strictly, one must not speak of new truths but of Christian truths newly minted. There was only newness in the presentation of the fourfold nature of Christian experience. Even so, this fresh light on truth as old as the Gospel, came with the force of a fresh discovery to multitudes, and there was a revival of religion because a coin lost in a corner had been found and freshly polished. If every true revival is, in essence, the re-capturing of some neglected dogma, then the Methodist revival swept through the earth because two brothers discovered afresh the deathless love of God and the sweep of that love in the heart of the believer and in the family of the Church.

CHAPTER SIX

What Remains?

THERE REMAINS the Methodist Church; but that is a question-begging answer. Methodists form a world community of over thirty millions including adherents, and so the Methodist Church is one of the strongest and most influential Protestant Churches in the world. Nevertheless it does not conform to any fixed pattern. In the United States, where there is by far the largest of all Methodist Churches, it has a constitutional episcopacy, makes only a limited use of lay preachers, is not organized in any Circuit system parallel to that in Great Britain, and possesses its own distinctive *Book of Offices*. Despite the grouping of Churches and Districts, Conferences and jurisdictional areas, the majority of ministers in the United States are still pastors of one Church only. In other countries too great distances and sparsely populated areas have led to modifications of the original eighteenth-century organization.

Yet a Methodist, in spite of differences in polity, can still recognize the indisputable signs of a Methodist Church wherever he travels, and can know that 'the Methodist people are one people throughout the world'. There are four clues by which in any part of the world a man may know he is still in the Methodist family. They can be subsumed under the four headings of doctrine, discipline, liturgy, and polity.

Is there a recognizable difference in doctrinal emphasis between Methodists and Christians in other great Communions?

In a technological age, with its mass production, mass propaganda, and mass media of entertainment, people's palates are continually titillated with things new and ephemeral, and many of them know little or nothing of the Christian faith. They have not examined the Bible and found it false; they have not sought to pray and found it unreal; they have not come to church and found it outmoded; they have been otherwise occupied, and Bible, prayer and church-going have fallen into neglect. The people invited to the feast were most apologetic, but they had fields, oxen, and family life and therefore prayed to be excused. Their hands were full. So it is today.

Christians of all Churches must accept this challenge to their Faith, and among the things they need are vision and energy to free themselves from denominational blinkers and know their oneness in Christ Jesus. This awareness of themselves as members of the one body of Christ ought increasingly to involve all Christians, laymen as well as ministers and clergy, in common acts of worship, in intercommunion, in common pronouncements on social

WHAT REMAINS?

issues, and above all in a common evangelistic programme.

Whether one likes it or not, the outsider is not impressed when a divided Church speaks to a divided world. But if in factory and open-air work, or in visitation evangelism, the appeal is in the name of the one Church, so much greater is the success. The value of mass evangelism is a matter of controversy, but no one disputes that if it is to be effective it must be supported by all the main Communions.

There is a deep level where members of different Churches discover a unity transcending all differences. Because they hold the essential truths embodied in the Creeds about the Father, Son and Holy Spirit, the holy Catholic Church, the forgiveness of sins and the life everlasting, they share a common experience. Since for all Christians there is the one Lord, the one Faith, the one Baptism, the one Victory over sin and death, there is also the one language. 'The love of Jesus, what it is, None but His loved ones know', but they *do* know, and they all know, and fundamentally they all speak of the same thing. Matthew Arnold tells in one of his sonnets of the rapture of the nonconformist preacher in Spitalfields; Hugh Benson in a story tells of the rapture of the nun before the High Altar; and John Masefield describes the rapture of the drunken bully acknowledging the Everlasting Mercy. Those of whom these writers told differed widely in their

Christian allegiance, but all knew the peace which passes understanding, the power which makes men more than conquerors, the joy which nothing can disturb.

> *Ten thousand thousand are their tongues,*
> *But all their joys are one.*

In a profound sense therefore the Methodist of today is not to be distinguished from his counterpart in other Churches. Nevertheless this is only part of the truth, for even in the language of the saints there can be a difference of idiom and accent. The instructed Methodist is brought up on a theology of experience. Believing in the articles of the Creed, he emphasizes especially the relation of the Christian with his Lord, and in consequence with his fellows. Salvation by faith means for the Methodist that the King is Father, and that His 'sufficient, sovereign, saving grace' is but his love in action: ''Tis love! 'tis love! Thou diedst for me!' The grace is unbounded, the love is unlimited, and therefore it is for all. The distinguishing note of the *Methodist Hymn-book* is in the astonishing use of the small words 'me' and 'all':

> *Father of me and all mankind,*

and again:

> *Who did for every sinner die*
> *Hath surely died for me.*

But a love capable of forgiveness and deliverance cannot be earned; neither works nor merit will avail. It can only be received by faith, and that faith is, in John Wesley's words, 'a disposition of the heart, a recumbency on God'. It is now, as in Wesley's day, the loving response to the loving Father.

Furthermore the Methodist today is still taught from John Wesley's sermons, Charles Wesley's hymns, and the whole tradition of his Church, to accept the doctrine of 'assurance'. This is not the subjectivism of the feelings, because it rests upon the objective truths of the Christian Faith. It is the belief that God's Spirit witnesses with our spirit that we are the children of God, and that with the Spirit of adoption comes the knowledge that we are no longer servants but sons. In one of his early Conferences John Wesley defined this assurance as ease after pain, rest after labour, joy after sorrow, light after darkness. He was lighting up in his own fashion what Paul described as the fruit of the Spirit. This teaching gave the early Methodist a religious self-awareness; apart from the early Franciscan movement there has been no period in Christian history when this sense of deliverance and joy was so evident. And still the Methodist people can sing the rapturous hymns of Charles Wesley without embarrassment.

It is arguable that John Wesley's teaching on Christian Perfection no longer warms his people's hearts, despite his warning that 'where Scriptural holiness is not preached the societies languish'. One reason is that the doctrine of holiness has so largely become a monopoly of the splinter sects. But the Methodists still warm to John Wesley's description of the Spirit-filled life, 'loving God with heart and soul and strength and mind, and one's neighbour as oneself'. In the Bristol Conference of 1758 one question asked: 'What does Christian Perfection imply?' The answer was: 'Loving God with all the heart, so that every evil temper is destroyed, and every word and work springs from and is conducted to the end by the pure love of God and our neighbour.'

This is an approach to holiness which is rooted in New Testament teaching; it is as fresh as the morning and is validated in modern experience. Some of the most used and best loved hymns of modern Methodists are on Christian Holiness, and in searching modern books and articles by Methodist theologians in many countries the teaching on holiness is being freshly minted.

Finally, today as much as ever, the Methodist people stress the Wesleyan teaching about fellowship. It is true that just as the Parisian mobs who precipitated the French Revolution had little knowledge of Rousseau save for one or two catch-phrases which they made their own, so modern Methodists have little first-hand acquaintance with John Wesley's writings apart from one or two sayings which have

WHAT REMAINS?

moulded their outlook. But they know that John Wesley looked upon the world as his parish, that he declared the Methodist people to be the friends of all and the enemies of none, that he discovered that the Bible knows nothing of solitary religion, and that he held that all holiness is social holiness. The well-known sayings are few, but the purport of them is plain. It is not John, however, but his brother who has largely conditioned the Methodist people to rejoice in their fellowship with each other and the wider family of God. Charles Wesley's hymns on the Communion of Saints, for example, are not easily paralleled in any other hymn-book in Christendom.

The Methodist people have also been trained for two centuries to think ecumenically. Before the eighteenth century was out Methodism had been established in North America and the West Indies, and soon, in its eastward look, was to come to Ceylon, India and the Isles of the Pacific. In the nineteenth and twentieth centuries Methodist Missions have covered the globe. Charles Wesley taught Methodists to sing that the whole earth was within the empire of God's love and that His undistinguishing regard was cast on Adam's fallen race. Small wonder that world Methodism is one of the largest and most virile of confessional Churches and that the World Methodist Council and the Quinquennial World Methodist Conferences are only the outward signs of an inner unity of spirit. In a letter within a year of his death, John Wesley wrote: 'It is expedient that the Methodists in every part of the globe should be united together as closely as possible. That we may all be one is the prayer of your affectionate friend and brother.' Today Methodists know that they are one family in the earth.

This Methodist teaching about fellowship does not mean, as 'some fellows of the baser sort' assert, that the Methodist is bounded by the limits of the Methodist family. In Methodist Churches of all countries there has been warm support of the World Council of Churches and its world assemblies; in the national and local Councils of Christian Churches Methodists play their proper part. But how far, it may be asked, is this true of generals rather than privates? The answer must be that Methodist laity lag behind no others, but that throughout the Christian Church the vision and initiative of leaders must increasingly be shared by the rank and file.

The second vital element in the outlook of Methodist people today is their sense of social responsibility. John Wesley was not only a great evangelist, but the most public-spirited citizen and the first social reformer of his day. When the *Gentleman's Magazine* and the *Monthly Review* published their obituary notices, they concentrated on the 'extensive good' Wesley had done for 'the lower classes in the community'.

WHAT REMAINS?

The General Rules drawn up by John and Charles Wesley for the use of Methodists and published in 1743 were flexible in expression and yet binding in their nature. They have given a certain definition to Methodist behaviour for two hundred years. Now they have become so much a part of the Methodist way of life that Methodists are moulded by them without knowing of their existence. There were three general rules for living. People who wished to come into the Methodist Society had only one condition to fulfil—'a desire to flee from the wrath to come and to be saved from their sins'. But the Wesleys maintained that the sincerity of this desire could be shown only by 'fruits'. They declared, therefore, that Methodists should continue to evidence their desire of salvation—

First, by doing no harm, by avoiding evil in every kind especially that which is most generally practised.

Secondly, by doing good, by being in every kind, merciful after their power; as they have opportunity, doing good of every possible sort, and as far as possible, to all men.

Thirdly, by attending upon all the ordinances of God. Such are the public worship of God; the ministry of the word, either read or expounded; the Supper of the Lord; family and private prayer; searching the Scriptures; and Fasting or abstinence.

In a word, Methodists were to do no harm, to do good, and to use the means of grace.

It is true that the Methodist people may sometimes be suspected of a social creed consisting only of abstinence from drink, gambling and irregular sex behaviour. This criticism stands self-exposed, for no world Church possesses so large a corpus of social teaching, or year by year makes such authoritative pronouncements through its various Conferences in many countries on public issues of the day. The instructed Methodist in any country knows that even his negatives are in the interest of a positive affirmation about life. He denounces anti-social habits and the vested interests which exploit them, because he seeks a realm of joyous living in which no hurtful thing can find a place. At his best the Methodist everywhere is evangelical in experience and social in outlook.

In world Methodism there is not only a general abstinence from all social evils which are either wrong in themselves or harmful from their first consequences, but a quite remarkable humanitarianism which shows itself in the building of hospitals, homes for old people and convalescents, orphanages, homes for delinquent youth, schools and colleges. The list of social welfare activities differs in certain particulars in different countries according to need and opportunity, but always, wherever Methodists associate together, there is the active disposition to seek the general good. This is an 'activism' not to be scorned, for it is a sensitive understanding of the

WHAT REMAINS?

'Inasmuch' warning which Jesus gave to all His followers.[1]

Thirdly, there is the liturgy which distinguishes Methodists throughout the world. This is not to be found in the Watchnight, Love-feast, and Covenant Services, distinctive as they are, for these may differ in emphasis and observance in different places. It is not to be found in a *Book of Offices,* for though world Methodism in its administration of the Sacraments and its services for marriage and burial bears the indubitable marks of its Anglican heritage, and though Adam Clarke said 'had it not been under God for this blessed book, the liturgy of the British Church, I verily believe Methodism had never existed', the forms of service now in use are not everywhere the same. Nor is it to be found in the Methodist devotional literature which has helped to communicate our doctrines and to shape our liturgical practice. In the last resort, as Bernard Manning so well understood, our distinctive liturgy is in the hymns of Charles Wesley. Manning's words can bear endless quotation: 'You talk much, and you talk rightly, of the work Methodism does for the world and for the universal Church: but your greatest—incomparably your greatest—contribution to the common heritage of Christendom is in Wesley's hymns. All the other things which you do, others have done and can do as well, better, or less well.

[1] See Matthew 25:31-46.

But in Wesley's hymns you have something unique, no one else could have done it, and unless you preserve it for the use of all the faithful, till that day when we are all one, we shall all lose some of the best gifts of God. I implore you then, in these days when you are tempted to look at other parts of the Church and to dwell on your likeness to them and on the great things that we all have in common, keep that good thing committed peculiarly to your charge. This is your vineyard: do not come one day saying, "Whatever I have done elsewhere, mine own vineyard have I not kept". In Wesley's hymns, not divorced from the great tunes of the Handel tradition, you have what only you understand and what (I sometimes fear) you no longer think it worth while to understand.

'You may think my language about the hymns extravagant; therefore I repeat it in stronger terms. This little book—some 750 hymns[2]—ranks in Christian literature with the Psalms, the Book of Common Prayer, the Canon of the Mass. In its own way, it is perfect, unapproachable, elemental in its perfection. You cannot alter it except to mar it; it is a work of supreme devotional art by a religious genius. You may compare it with Leonardo's "Last Supper" or King's Chapel; and, as Blackstone said of the English Constitution, the proper attitude to take to it is this: we must venerate where we are not able presently to comprehend.'

[2] Wesley's Collection in 1780 has only 525 hymns.

WHAT REMAINS?

The hymns rightly used give form to our worship as they give substance to our thought. Their use differs greatly in different countries and among different individuals in the same country, but here is the greatest single treasure we can bring to the universal Church. Here, incomparably, may still be found suitable hymns for 'believers rejoicing, fighting, praying, watching, working, suffering, groaning for full redemption, brought to the birth, saved and interceding the world'. Here likewise the Church may find its fitting hymns for 'meeting, giving thanks, praying and parting'.

Finally there is the distinctive Methodist polity which remains as our legacy. Methodist Churches in many parts of the world have discarded important features of that connexionalism which showed John Wesley to be the master builder, but two great elements have not been allowed to go. The first is the type of Methodism's organization. If there be historically three great types of Church organization, Catholic, Presbyterian, and Congregational, then it is on the Presbyterian model that Methodist Churches are fashioned. They neither desire the exclusiveness of the Catholic nor the independency of the Congregationalist. They recognize with John Wesley that the strong must help the weak, and that the Church in its central organization must help to succour and maintain its separate parts. So in Methodism everywhere there is centralization combined with local

SONS TO SAMUEL

autonomy and enterprise. The principle of belonging to one another has been interpreted in ecclesiastical terms.

The second element is the continuing importance of the laity. From the beginning no Church has made better use of its laymen. John Wesley thought of his Society much as Ignatius Loyola conceived his Society of Jesus. It was to be an order within the Church, and therefore he was ready to use all its members. By dint of borrowing ideas and brilliant improvisation, Wesley used his people as preachers, class leaders, trustees, and stewards of local societies.

In the next century, chiefly through agitation and secession, the power and functions of the laity increased.

In America the great westward movement of the Methodist Church could not have taken place without the energy, courage and devotion of laymen. Francis Asbury was the great precursor of a veritable host of dauntless Circuit-riders, but he and they alike depended upon the laymen in the lonely outposts to sustain and develop the work. The whole history of Methodism in Australia and New Zealand has been the conquest of vast spaces through the team-work of minister and layman. In the record of Methodist Overseas Missions, success or failure can be estimated by the way laymen have been brought into the councils and actions of the Church. There is no layman whose gifts cannot be fully used

WHAT REMAINS?

both in the administrative and purely spiritual aspects of the Church's work; the Reformation stress on the priesthood of all believers is finely expressed in this eager use of the layman's gifts and energies. Modern complaints are never that we fail to use laymen, but only that too few laymen allow themselves to be used.

Just as there is no such creature as the 'average man', so there is no such creature as the typical Methodist. Nevertheless, if one could suppose such a person to exist, he would be a devoted member of his Church, occupying such offices as were suitable to his age and abilities. He would maintain friendly relations with other Christians of other Churches and take an active interest in Methodism overseas and in the world-wide Church. He would be a good family man, a keen and co-operative worker in his daily employment, and a respected citizen eagerly sharing in community life. Above all, he would use the means of grace to nourish his sense of God's presence and his resolve to walk in God's way. At his best he would be a troubadour of God, because with all God's merry men in all ages he would know the cause of joy unspeakable:

> *The heart that believes*
> *His Kingdom receives,*
> *His power and His peace,*
> *His life, and His joy's everlasting increase.*

If someone objects that that is a description of

every believer, let it be acknowledged that it is so. Was it not Heine who said a man is always right in what he affirms and wrong in what he denies? What can be asserted safely is that the people called Methodists have a special responsibility for this sort of living. It is safeguarded in their doctrinal standards, defined in their discipline, expressed in their liturgy, and worked out in their polity. Wesley himself gave clarity to this Methodist way of life, and the last interpretative word must lie with him:

'If you walk by this rule, continually endeavouring to know and love and resemble and obey the great God and Father of our Lord Jesus Christ, as the God of Love and pardoning mercy; if from this principle of loving, obedient faith, you carefully abstain from all evil, and labour, as you have opportunity, to do good to all men, friends or enemies; if, lastly, you unite together, to encourage and help each other in thus working out your salvation, and for that end watch over one another in love, you are they whom I mean by Methodists.'

Happy are they who walk by such a rule.

Index

Aldersgate Street, 58
America, 46, 49, 130
American Independence, War of, 37, 46
American Indians, 24
Anglican Church, 16, 19, 20, 22, 23, 38, 97
Annesley, Samuel, 6, 98
Asbury, Francis, 46, 130
Athenian Oracle, 14
Axholme, 1

Bath, 45
Baptism, 112
Barratt, Rev. T. H., 22
Beaumont, Dr, 20
Böhler, Peter, 57, 60, 98
Bray, Mr, 59
Bristol, 41, 62, 79
Broughton, Thomas, 53
Burton, Dr, 54
Butler, Bishop, 65

Calvin, John, 12, 85, 88
Calvinism, 15, 87, 88
Catholic, Roman, 19, 116, 129
Chandler, Dr, 47, 48
Charity School, 22
Charterhouse, 27, 50
Christ Church, 26, 50
Church of England, 20, 41, 42, 80, 97
Clarke, Adam, 81, 127
Coke, Thomas, 46, 79
Congregationalism, 15, 129
Couch, Quiller, A., 3
Cownley, Joseph, 41

Deists, 13
Dissenters, 42, 47

Dissertations on Job, 9, 11

Epworth, 1, 6, 29, 38

Foundery, 76

Gambold, John, 52, 54
Gentleman's Magazine, 7, 124
Georgia, 24, 35, 38, 49, 53, 54, 62

Hervey, James, 54
Holland, William, 57
Holy Club, 33, 34, 52
Holy Communion, 2
Hutton, Mrs, 22

Ingham, Benjamin, 53, 54.

Jacobite, 22
Johnson, Dr Samuel, 7

Kingswood, 22
Kirkham, Betty and Sarah, 52

Leeds Conference, 43
Lincoln College, 28, 33
Liturgy, 127
London, 75, 76, 77, 79
Luther, Martin, 11, 85-88

McNab, Mr, 45
Methodism, modern, 117ff.
Methodist Revival, 16, 49, 60, 84
Methodist Societies, 23
Missionary work, 123
Moravianism, 53, 57, 62, 90, 98
Munchin, Joe, 71
Murray, Grace, 41, 49
Music, 17

SONS TO SAMUEL

Notes on the New Testament, 11
Notes on the Life of Christ, 14

Oglethorpe, General, 24, 36, 54
Open-air preaching, 63
Oxford University, 9, 27, 33, 34, 49, 62
Oxford, Bishop of, 18, 36

Perronet, Charles Edward, 42, 44
Presbyterian, 97, 112, 129

Rectory, the, 3, 25
Reformation, 85, 99, 163
Renaissance, 85, 90

Sacraments, 53, 77, 127
St Ives, 72
Sellon, Rev. Walter, 42
Southey, Robert, 39, 66
Spectator, The, 28
Stanton Rectory, 51

Tindal, Nicholas, 12
Tiverton Grammar School, 27
Toland, John, 12
Turner, Mrs, 59
Tyerman, Luke, 14

Unitarianism, 14

Walpole, Sir Robert, 27
Watts, Isaac, 193
Wednesbury Riots, 68, 71
Wesley's Chapel, 76
Wesley, Charles—
  Bristol years, 74, 83
  controversy with preachers, 77
  conversion, 56-61
  early years, 5, 26, 50
  family life, 75
  Georgia, 35, 54, 56
  hymns, 10, 12, 17, 83, 90, 93, 100, 107, 123
  illness and death, 81
  London Methodism, 76, 78, 79, 83
  marriage, 74
  ordinations, 46f.
  Oxford, 50
  relations with John, 21, 35, 36, 43
  relations with Samuel, 33, 37, 40
  riots, 69, 73
Wesley, Hetty, 7, 29
Wesley, John—
  conversion, 56-61
  early years, 5, 10, 20, 26, 34, 50
  Epworth household, 29
  Georgia, 35, 54-6
  George Whitefield, 63
  Oxford, 23, 50, 52
  Peter Böhler, 56, 57
  relations with Charles, 21, 36, 44, 48, 76, 84
  relations with colonists, 55
  relations with preachers, 77
  relations with Samuel, 27, 28, 30, 32, 38
  Teaching of Assurance, 15, 22, 31, 89, 92, 95-9, 121
  Teaching of Fellowship, 92, 108
  Teaching of Holiness, 89, 92, 103, 122
  Teaching of Salvation, 89, 92, 94
  Teaching of Work of Holy Spirit, 114-16
Wesley, Samuel, father, 5-25, 53, 98
Wesley, Samuel, son, 10, 16, 21, 26, 27, 35, 50
Wesley, sisters, 7
Wesley, Susanna, 6, 14, 19, 98
Westminster School, 26, 27, 33, 50
Whitefield, George, 22, 54, 55-63
Wroot, 29

www.ingramcontent.com/pod-product-compliance
Lightning Source LLC
Chambersburg PA
CBHW071510150426
43191CB00009B/1472